Unlocking the Scriptures for You

HEBREWS

A Bible Study on Hebrews

By

David L. Eubanks and Robert C. Shannon

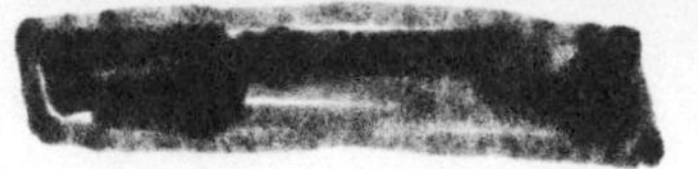

ISBN: 1-4140-4111-X (e-book)
ISBN: 1-4140-4110-1 (Paperback)

This book is printed on acid free paper.

Sharing the thoughts of his own heart, the author may express views not entirely consistent with those of the publisher.

1stBooks - rev. 12/31/03

CONTENTS

FOREWORD

This book is unlike any other you'll find. Not that you won't find a number of good studies on the book of Hebrews; there are several available. But this is different. It's not a commentary, but it does "comment" on the text of Hebrews in a passage-by-passage treatment. Nor is it a topical study, although several "topics" are discussed.

What makes this book different is its two-level approach to the book of Hebrews. The first level is the passage-by-passage exegesis of the text of Hebrews. This portion was done by David L. Eubanks, President of Johnson Bible College near Knoxville, Tennessee. His brief but insightful comments will help you grasp the theme of the book of Hebrews as well as understand many of the specific points that are made.

The second level is the illustrative exegesis found at the end of each chapter. Titled "Lessons From Chapter—," each of these sections points out practical applications of the ideas contained in the preceding section. Robert C. Shannon has contributed these lessons, and he's filled them with the powerful illustrations for which he is so well known. Before retiring in the beautiful mountains of North Carolina, Bob served as a pastor, Bible college professor, and missionary behind the Iron Curtain.

If you are serious about studying the book of Hebrews, this book is for you. You'll find here some easy-to-understand explanations of the themes in Hebrews, the historical and cultural context, and how the book relates to other passages. And you'll find practical application of these truths to your own life.

If you are a Sunday-school teacher, teaching youth or adults, this book is for you. Here you'll find easy explanations of sometimes obscure passages. You'll have help in answering your students' questions in clear, easy terms. The illustrations will make your lessons sparkle.

If you are a preacher wanting to preach from Hebrews, this book is for you. Whether you're preaching a series from Hebrews or just one or two sermons, this book will provide valuable insights on your text. In fact, the "Lessons" section that concludes each chapter almost always suggests a sermon outline all by itself. Suppose you're preaching from Hebrews 10, particularly the last half of the chapter. The subheads in "Lessons From Chapter Ten" suggest a simple three-point outline: the Assurance of Faith, the Profession of Faith, and the Expression of Faith.

Would you like to lead a home Bible study? Again, this book is for you. This study will provide for three full months of rich Bible study (meeting once-a-week.

If you are a Christian, if you want to know your Lord more intimately, then this book is for you. I highly recommend this study of Hebrews for everyone who wants deeper insight into the message of Hebrews but doesn't have the time to spend in a library digging for it himself. By itself or as a supplement to your study, this book will enrich your life.

—The Editor

INTRODUCTION

Authorship

Possibly no book in the New Testament has more legitimate introductory problems connected with its study than the epistle to the Hebrews. Although the authorship of Paul has been traditionally associated with the work, there is no clear indication as to the author within the letter itself. The title in many of our English Bibles, "The Epistle of Paul the Apostle to the Hebrews," is not a part of any original manuscript. Tertullian suggested Barnabas as the writer. Martin Luther thought Apollos wrote it, and John Calvin's choice of author was Luke. Perhaps the most certain and incontrovertible word on the subject was Origen's assertion, "As to who wrote the Epistle, the truth is known to God." Any reader who clings to the Pauline authorship can feel justified in doing so, assured that he has much sound scholarship on his side. He should realize, however, that the integrity of this great treatise does not rest upon his or any other man's opinion concerning the human author of Hebrews.

Date

Concerning the date of composition, this letter could hardly have been written later than A.D. 96, for in that year, Clement of Rome alluded to it in his epistle to the Corinthians. In fact, it was probably written before A.D. 70, inasmuch as the author did not refer to the destruction of Jerusalem, which occurred in that year. Also, he used the present tense in referring to the offering of Jewish sacrifices (particularly in 9:6-9), as if such practices were still going on. At the same time, however, there are indications that the epistle was written later than most of the other letters in the New Testament. Chief among these is the certain implication that the Hebrews were second-generation Christians. (See 5:12 and 10:32-39.) The probable date is sometime between A.D. 67 and 69.

Destination

Suggestions for the possible destination of the treatise have included Jerusalem, Alexandria, Antioch, Ephesus, Rome, Caesarea, and Samaria. Many scholars argue that the likeliest home of the readers was Rome and that "they of Italy," referred to in 13:24, were Italian Christians living elsewhere who wished to send greetings to their friends back home.

Purpose

There is some debate among the scholars concerning the author's purpose. Whether it was to prevent Jewish Christians from returning to Judaism, or to present the worldwide scope of the Christian religion to Jewish Christians who had been reluctant to recognize the same, the fact remains that much of the letter represents a treatment of the superiority of Christianity over Judaism. Having left Judaism for Christianity a long time back, they were in danger of growing weary of the new system. They apparently could not see enough difference between the two religions to endure continued persecution for their faith. In fact, it may very well be that they thought Judaism actually excelled over Christianity in some points. Therefore, the Hebrews writer was compelled to demonstrate that Christianity is not only superior to Judaism; it is also God's purposed completion of the same.

The Writer's Introduction (1:1-4)

The purpose of the writer's introduction is to illustrate the exalted name and position of Jesus Christ and to present the reasons for His deserving such a position. In the very first chapter, the stage is set for what will follow in the rest of the book. In accord with this purpose, the author treated Jesus' place in revelation and His relationship to God, to the universe, and to the angels. Discussing Jesus' place in revelation, he not only stressed the difference between our Lord as God's final revelation and all other revelations that had gone before (such as dreams, visions, preaching, dramatizing, and states of ecstasy), he also affirmed that all previous revelations had pointed to Jesus as God's ultimate one. God's Son was the climax of a long series of revelations by God. Divine revelation is thus seen to be progressive. The coming of Christ was prepared for by continued revelation of God through the Old Testament. He was the end toward which everything else had moved.

"In these last days," God chose to disclose himself through His Son. Matthew (1:23) quoted from Isaiah 7:14 when he said that Mary's son would be called Emmanuel, or "God with us." The eternal God had stepped into the pages of history. Since the only complete revelation of truth has to be in personality, when God chose to reveal himself completely, He chose a personality, His only Son. As God's Son, Christ was the brightness of His glory, the stamp of God's character. He radiated the glory of the Father in such a way that men saw it. He presented the fullness of God in such a way that men could understand it.

As God's Son, Christ was the instrument of universal creation. This same assertion was made by other New Testament writers, such as John, who said, "Through him all things were made; without him nothing was made that has been made" (John 1:3). Paul wrote, "All things were created by him and for him" (Colossians 1:16).

Not limited to creation alone, Jesus' power extends even to the sustaining and redeeming of this universe as well. He is the one in whom "all things hold together" (Colossians 1:17). Thus he deserves to be "heir [Lord] of all things" and to hold a place of honor at the right hand of the Father.

Part One:

The Preeminence of Christ

CHAPTER ONE

Superior to the Angels

Hebrews 1:5-2:4

The Premise Stated (1:5-14)

The author of Hebrews compared Christ to the angels in order to lay the foundation for his argument that Christianity is superior to Judaism. Although today's average Gentile reader doesn't realize it, the Jew believed that the Old Testament law (and thus his religion) was given by angels. (See Acts 7:35; Galatians 3:19; Hebrews 2:2.) The writer therefore began his comparison of the two ages, or the two religious systems, by contrasting their messengers, the angels in the one case, and the Son in the other.

In order to illustrate that Jesus Christ is preeminent over the angels, the Hebrews author quoted from the Old Testament. He showed first that God asserted Jesus to be His Son, and himself to be Jesus' Father, a declaration that He never made of any of the angels (Hebrews 1:6; Psalm 2:7; 2 Samuel 7:14). Then he said that the angels were even commanded to worship Jesus (Hebrews 1:6; Psalm 97:7). Next, the writer said that God clothes the angels in any form, even material (winds, flames of fire), to serve Him. Jesus, who is called God, has His throne established forever and ever (Hebrews 1:7, 8; Psalm 45:6; 104:4). Fourth. the writer showed that God anointed Jesus above the angels (Hebrews 1:9; Psalm 45:7). Then he pointed out that Christ, as Lord, laid the foundations of the world, and the angels are merely the work of His hands (Hebrews 1:10; Psalm 102:25). The writer went on to say that the world decays and changes, but Jesus Christ remains the same forever (Hebrews 1:11, 12; Psalm 102:26, 27). Finally, he noted that God asked Christ to sit on His right hand, while the angels are sent forth as servants to serve "those who will inherit salvation" (Hebrews 1:13, 14; Psalm 110:1).

By referring to Psalms and other Old Testament passages, the Hebrew writer was able to show the Jewish Christians that Jesus Christ, the revealer of Christianity, is above the angels. The Old Testament, as well as the New, teaches that Christ has a more excellent name and a more exalted position than the angels. Through the Scriptures, the writer was able to demonstrate that the angels are of no interest in themselves. While they were mediators of the revelation that foreshadowed the Christian age, even they must pay homage to the Son, who is the fulfillment of this revelation. Thus the

Christian age, or the age of redemption, is as much higher than the Old Testament as the Son is greater than the angels.

Warning and Admonition (2:1-4)

Having shown the superiority of Christ to the angels, and thus of the new order to the old, the Hebrews writer proceeded to warn his readers to regard seriously the authority and finality of the truth of God's Son and admonish them against drifting from Him. He declared that a breach of the law of Moses, which was mediated by angels and expressed only in concealed form the purpose of God, resulted in certain and severe punishment. How, then, could one hope to escape God's wrath when he disregarded the promised word of salvation delivered by Christ himself, confirmed by those who heard Him, and attested to by miracles? It is a foolish member of the church who supposes that one under grace has a lesser obligation than one under the law.

Lessons From Chapter One

In 1944, C.E. Goodman of Hallmark Greeting Cards wrote a slogan: "When You Care Enough to Send the Very Best." Ever since, that motto has been used to sell greeting cards. By changing the slogan slightly, it becomes a capsule of this whole section of Scripture: "When God Cared Enough to Send the Very Best."

God Spoke Through His Son (1:1, 2).

The chapter begins with a long and involved sentence. However, the sentence can be shortened to get at its heart. The heart is this: *"God spoke through His Son."* We are amazed that God speaks to us at all. We should not be surprised if He were as silent as Buddha, with his frozen smile and impassive face. No sound ever comes from his throat. But God has spoken.

We ought to listen when God speaks through His prophets. They were chosen by Him. They courageously gambled their lives on their message. Their prophecies were confirmed by history. We ought to listen when God speaks through His prophets.

We ought to listen when God speaks through angels. Chapter 2 begins by reminding us that "the message spoken by angels was binding." Angels spoke at Bethlehem at the birth of Christ. Angels spoke at the tomb at the resurrection of Christ. We ought to listen when God speaks through angles.

But how much more emphatically it can be said that we ought to listen when God speaks through His Son.

Synesthesia is the rare ability to perceive words in colors. There are only a few people who have this gift. It is not a case of being psychotic, or drunk, or drugged. It is an actual phenomenon. Richard Cytowic, a Washington, D.C., neurologist, has made an extensive study of this phenomenon. For people who have this gift, sounds are seen as well as heard. Harsh words, for example, might be perceived as dark and ugly. If one had such a gift, how would the words of God be seen? Would they be brilliant as gold? Would they be perceived in the crimson of Calvary, the blue of loyalty, the white of purity? Whether we have this rare gift or not, all of us need to listen when God speaks.

God Is Seen in His Son (1:3)

"No one has ever seen God," says the Bible (John 1:18). He is described as "eternal, immortal, invisible." Philip (in John 19:8) is speaking for all of us when he asks Jesus, "Show us the Father." It is not mere idle curiosity that makes us want to see God. It is not merely some academic quest for knowledge. From the deepest levels of our being, we want to see God. Hear Jesus: "Anyone who has seen me has seen the Father" (John 14:9). Hear Hebrews declare that the Son is "the express image of his person!" (1:3, KJV).

God is seen in nature, but only partially. We see fragments of God in nature. We see Him fully in His Son. We see Him clearly in His Son. We could see Him in ourselves, for we are made in His image; but we do not see Him clearly in ourselves. We see God accurately only in the Son. So much of our knowledge has proven to be inaccurate. This is true of our knowledge of heaven, the earth, the human body, the mind, and medicine. It is always serious when our knowledge is inaccurate. It is most serious when our knowledge of God is inaccurate.

"He's the image of his father," we say of someone's son. It may be that they look just alike, but still the son has his own personal individuality. Jesus is not God's Son in the same way that earthly sons are the image of earthly fathers. Jesus is God so that when God sent His Son, He sent himself.

God Rules Through His Son

Hebrews 1:8 says, "But about the Son he says, "Your throne, O God, will last for ever and ever." Recently, *"Omni"* magazine had an article entitled "When God Plays Dice with the Universe." Subtitled "Connosieurs of Chaos," the article described a new field of scientific inquiry. The basic premise is that there is a randomness built into the universe. Not everything is as orderly or as mechanistic as has been assumed. Chance is a part of the universe and, even if we had all the data, we could not always predict the outcome. Whether the connosieurs of chaos are right or not, certainly God does not play dice with the universe. He rules it; and He rules it through His Son. He rules the material world. Someday He will rule over all. "He must reign," says Paul, "until he has put all his enemies under his feet" (1 Corinthians 15:25). The Book of Revelation adds that "the kingdom of the world has become the kingdom of our Lord and of His Christ" (Revelation 11:15). Since He must eventually rule over all, He ought to rule now in the church—and in our lives!

God Redeems Through His Son (1:3)

Since God is infinite, He must have had many means at His disposal; but He chose to save through His Son. We don't know why, but we can guess. Perhaps it was to show His love. Perhaps it was to touch our hearts. Perhaps it was to give us an example. Whatever the reason, God chose to save through His Son. He saves only through Christ. He saves through Christ alone. "When he had *by himself* purged our sins ..." (Hebrews 1:3, KJV). Salvation is not a joint effort of man's work and God's grace! All who are saved are saved only by Christ and by Christ alone!

Henry J. Heimlich is the Cincinnati physician who developed the Heimlich maneuver. You've read about it. If a person is choking, you hug him sharply from behind, forcing your fist into his abdomen. A column of air is forced up and out, dislodging the obstruction. It is estimated that six thousand lives have been saved by the Heimlich maneuver. Millions have been saved by the Son.

McDonald's restaurants put up a sign declaring that so many billion McDonald's hamburgers have been served. What if we could have a sign in front of every church proclaiming the millions who have now been saved by the Son!

Conclusion

Since Hebrews 2:1 includes the word *therefore,* we know that it is really the conclusion to chapter one. The conclusion is twofold: hear and heed. "We must pay more careful attention, therefore, to what we have heard." Sometimes we do not even hear. "Jesus calls us, o'er the tumult of our life's wild restless sea." But we don't hear. Perhaps it is because our ears are blocked with the wax of the world. Perhaps it is because we have heard it so often that we really do not hear it at all. If you were to spend the night at my house, you probably would be kept awake by my clock, which chimes every quarter hour. However, I have heard it so often that I never hear it at all—*unless I want to!* But it is never enough just to hear. We must heed. Jesus said to hear and not to do was to build your house on the sand. To hear and to do was to build your house on the rock.

> Some build their hopes on the ever drifting sand;
> Some on their fame or their treasure or their land;
> Mine's on the Rock that forever shall stand,
> Jesus the "Rock of Ages."

CHAPTER TWO

Superior as Man

Hebrews 2:5-18

The purpose of this chapter is to show the reasonableness and necessity of Christ's becoming a man. If He was so much higher than the angels, as the Hebrews writer stressed so forcefully in the preceding context, why did He come wrapped in a mantle of human flesh? Some scholars would suggest that the very fact that Christ became a human being proves that He was, in fact, lower than the angels.

Man and Christ, Made a Little Lower Than the Angels (2:5-9)

In explaining the plausibility of our Lord's incarnation, the author of Hebrews appealed first to Psalm 8, to show that it was God's intended purpose that man, not angels, have universal dominion and occupy the highest place among God's creatures. (See Genesis 1:26.) Our Maker reserved glory and honor for man; but, because of sin and death, God's purpose was thwarted and man became anything but the respected ruler of creation. He was cut off from God's glory by his own weakness and failure.

Then the Man Jesus Christ came, made "for a little while lower[1] than the angels, to endure our humiliation and death. On account of Jesus' suffering and sacrifice, God exalted Him to a place of honor and praise as the ruler of the "world to come," the kingdom of God. (See Philippians 2:7-9.) Coronation followed humiliation. Thus the Messiah became the true fulfillment of what the Father intended man to be, and so opened the way for us to experience the glory and honor that our Creator meant for us.

The Savior Completely Identified With Man (2:10-13)

In His humiliation and suffering, Jesus Christ completely identified with man. Having shared fully in flesh and blood and having experienced completely the human predicament, He is perfectly qualified to sympathize with us as the pioneer of our salvation. Is it any wonder that He considers himself in the deepest sense our brother?

---

[1] Psalm 8:5, Septuagint

To further demonstrate the necessity of Jesus' suffering and His complete identification with His people, the writer of Hebrews appealed to three Old Testament passages: (1) Psalm 22:22 is a verse from a most familiar chapter of prophecy concerning the crucifixion of Jesus. This reference is to the relationship between the suffering Savior and His "brethren," the members of the church. (2) Isaiah 8:17 obviously refers to Isaiah, who, experiencing the rejection of his message and the discouragement that followed, confessed his dependence upon God. But it also points to Jesus, who so identified with man's sufferings that He shared the same dependence. (3) Isaiah 8:18, although immediately referring to the Hebrew prophet and his children, has ultimate application to Christ and His people. His identification with them in flesh and blood was so close that they can even be considered His children, a relationship mentioned in this epistle alone in all the New Testament.

The Destruction of the Fear of Death (2:14-16)

Still another (perhaps the main) reason for Christ's partaking of flesh and blood was to share in death and so deliver mankind from its power. This "power" is not the power that belonged to death itself, but the power that Satan possessed through death. The devil, using his chief weapon, death, did all that he could to conquer Jesus, but it was not enough. Our Lord's victory transformed death into an opportunity for blessing for man. (See 1 Corinthians 15:26, 54-57; 2 Timothy 1:10.) As one of the angels, who are out of the reach of death, Jesus could not have accomplished such a victory. Only as a man could He have done it.

Christ, the Compassionate High Priest (2:17, 18)

The Hebrews writer concluded chapter 2 with a brief introduction of the most important theme of his treatise, the high-priestly ministry of our Lord. The high priest was a servant of God and of the people. Jesus fulfilled both these roles. Having experienced man's temptation and suffering, He was able to sympathize completely with His people. At the same time, through His death, He offered sacrifice to God for their sins. The gulf between man and God was bridged through Jesus.

Thus the Hebrews writer has presented from Scripture and sound reasoning a brief but convincing case for the necessity of our Lord's humanity. As the only human being who ever fulfilled God's intended purpose for mankind's glory, Christ pioneered the way for all of us to fulfill

God's plan for man. To be a brother to those whom He was to save, He had to become one with them.

Jesus' destruction of the fear of death for all mankind was unavoidably contingent upon His own death as one of us. And His role as our compassionate and understanding high priest rested on His sharing the hardships, temptations, and bitter experiences of human life. Let us thank God that His Son was willing to experience such humiliation for us.

Lessons From Chapter Two

We Three Kings!

To mention such a phrase is to think of Christmas and the beloved Christmas hymn, "We Three Kings." There are three kings in the second chapter of Hebrews, but they have nothing to do with the Wisemen. The heart of the chapter is Christ, the King of Kings. Alongside Him, we see man, to whom God gave dominion over all that He had created. Then, by contrast, we see the devil, who has usurped God's power and is described in Scripture as the prince of this world.

The Majesty of Man

He was made only a little lower than the angels. Sometimes, if you want someone to do you a favor, you may say, "Be an angel." Florida has a State Repertory Theater company based in Sarasota, Florida. They take their name from the restored Italian theater in which they play—Asolo Theater. People who contribute to the ongoing of the program are called Asolo Angels.

Once, a minister who went to visit a couple newly married. He knocked at the front door. A feminine voice from within called out, "Is that you, angel?" "No," said the minister, "but I'm from the same department!"

We may not be angels, but we are from the same department.

There is much that is angelic about us. We, too, are His messengers. (That's what the word *angel* really means.) We have some limitations that angels do not. We have some advantages that angels do not. The Bible says that angels sin, but nowhere does it say that God provided any remedy for angels' sins. God has provided a remedy for our sin! So we may be lower than the angels, but we are only a little lower than the angels. We are to have dominion over all the created universe. When modern man first tried rain-making, some said he was over stepping himself. No! WE have dominion over all the universe. It is no more a sin to make rain (if that is possible) than it is to dam rivers, dig canals, plant gardens, or pull weeds. Man is in charge.

The Condescension of Christ

Christ is the supreme King. Though man is far exalted above all other living things, Christ is far, far higher than man. He is so much higher that it was a great condescension for Him to come to earth. Simply to live on this little planet among us was a great condescension. Christ did more than that. He lived among us in human flesh. He felt cold and heat, pain and weariness. Deprive Him of food and He hungered. Deprive Him of water and He thirsted. It is worth noting that Jesus began His ministry hungering on the mount of temptation and ended His ministry thirsting on mount Calvary!

He went further than simply living in human flesh and suffering as humans suffer. He died as we die. Not only did He die, He died the most horrible and shameful death possible. Read Philippians 2:7-9 very carefully. To the world of the first century, such things seemed totally inappropriate for a King. The Hebrews writer says they were, in fact, most appropriate. "It was fitting," he writes in 2:10—or, in the KJV, "it became Him." If a dress particularly suits a woman, we say, "It's becoming." If a jacket particularly suits a man, we say, "It's becoming." So the Hebrews writer says it was becoming, fitting, appropriate that the King of Kings should endure the worst of earth.

Dr. John Rosen pioneered a new treatment for the severely mentally ill. There were some catatonic patients, people who took to their beds curled up in the fetal position and refused to acknowledge that anyone else even existed. They would neither move nor speak. Dr. Rosen moved in on the floor. He put up a cot there. Every day he would see the patients. Sometimes he would stop by a bed, take off his jacket and tie, and climb into bed with the patient. He would put his arms around him and gently embrace him. Some returned to the world of living because of that wordless expression of concern. Hebrews 2, Philippians 2, and the Christmas story as well tell us that in Christ, God moved in on the ward!

The Doom of the Devil

Is the devil a king? Do we have a right to place him here alongside man and Christ and speak of *three* kings? Yes! Jesus called the devil "the prince of this world" (John 12:31; 14:30; 16:11). If you do not believe the devil is the prince of this world, you have not been reading the newspapers! If you do not believe the devil is the prince of this world, you have not been watching the evening news! Drugs, alcohol, lust, and greed control lives by the millions. They are the devil's devices! They are his tools.

Recently, a study was made of advertising and the value of symbols. They determined that the most readily recognized symbol in America was the flag. The *fourth* most widely recognized symbol in America was the *Playboy* Bunny! Isn't that significant!

The devil has no right to rule over this world. He is a usurper. He takes the power that belongs to the other kings. He takes the power that belongs to man. He takes the power that belongs to Christ. Sometimes he takes men's power so completely that they lose all self-control. They do not sin because they may—they sin because they must! He puts hate in the heart where Christ would put love. He puts brutality in the heart where Christ would put mercy. He puts revenge in the heart where Christ would put forgiveness. But his rule is temporary. His doom is sure.

The brother of one of my ancestors died in the last battle of the American Revolution, the Battle of Blue Lick's. It was a battle that should never have been fought, for it was fought after the war was over! News traveled slowly in the wilderness. They had no quick means of communication. No one in the wilderness knew the victory had been won. He died in a battle fought after the victory had already been won. In a sense, Christ won the victory over the devil at Calvary and in His resurrection. All that was left after that was to proclaim the terms of the armistice—and to engage in some mopping up operations. But we are still seeing some battles fought. The devil does not take defeat easily. He continues to wound and kill. But the victory is already assured.

Someday the last battle will be fought, but already the war is won!

A favorite gospel song is "Victory In Jesus!" It is a stirring song, but the preposition *in* tells only part of the story. It is also a victory *by* Jesus and a *victory from* Jesus. As Paul says, "Thanks be to God! He *gives* us the victory through our Lord Jesus Christ" (1 Corinthians 15:57).

CHAPTER THREE

Greater Than Moses and Joshua

Hebrews 3:1-4:13

The Superiority of the Son to the Servant (3:1-6)

The Hebrews writer began chapter 3 on the same note with which he concluded the previous chapter, the twofold ministry of our Lord. He did this by focusing the attention of his readers on the apostleship and the high priesthood of Jesus. (Only in Hebrews are these terms used of Jesus.) Like Moses, Christ received God's appointment as both His ambassador to men and their representative to Him.

In the performance of His ministry, Christ was faithful, just as Moses had been. Of the Jewish lawgiver God himself had testified, "My servant Moses ... is faithful in all my house. With him I speak face to face" (Numbers 12:7, 8). There is no more inspiring story on record of a mediator's earnest intercession for others than the account of Moses' pleading for the children of Israel after they fell under God's judgment for worshiping the golden calf at Sinai. (See Exodus 31, 32.) And this incident does not represent the only example of Moses' spirited intercession for his people. The faithfulness of Moses is without contradiction.

Although they compare in their appointment by God and their fidelity to that commission, Christ is as uniquely superior to Moses as the builder of a house is greater than the house. Any architect is entitled to more honor than the building that he designs. Moses was only a part of the house, one of God's created beings, but Jesus was the Creator. Moreover, in the family of God, Christ deserves greater respect than Moses, just as a son holds a higher rank than a servant in the house. Jesus is the Son of God; Moses was a son of Abraham. The mediator of the Old Covenant was a servant (the respected leader, but still a servant) in the household, Israel. Christ, the Mediator of the New, is the Son who rules over the household, the church, spiritual Israel. (See Ephesians 2:19-22.)

Of course, the obvious conclusion is that the New Covenant inaugurated by Christ is preeminent to the Old Covenant instituted by Moses. As John wrote, "The law was given through Moses; grace and truth came through Jesus Christ" (John 1:17).

Warning Based on the Failure of Israel (3:7-19)

The first section of this chapter closed with an assurance to the readers that they would remain a part of this great family of God, over which Christ ruled, if they maintained their faith in Him and their faithfulness to Him. The writer continued into the remaining section by warning them that a rejection of God's Son would meet with even sterner judgment than Israel received in the wilderness under Moses. If Christ and His order are superior to Moses and the order ushered in by him, then it is absolutely necessary that we place our trust in Jesus and obey His voice.

In making a comparison between the failure of Israel and the consequences of lack of faith on the part of his readers, the Hebrews writer cited Psalm 95:7-11, a reference to two incidents from the wilderness journey of Israel under Moses. The first occurred at the beginning of their journey at Rephidim. Afraid of dying without water, the people complained bitterly to Moses and even expressed regret at having left Egypt and the security of the provisions that they had there. (See Exodus 17:1-7.)

The second experience took place when they reached Canaan at Kadesh-barnea and sent spies to examine the promised land. Although the returning scouts described the land as rich and prosperous, just as God had promised, the majority report was unfavorable to possessing the land because of the superior size and strength of the inhabitants. Accepting the recommendation of the spies, in opposition to the clear commandment of God, and again sighing for the shelter of oppressive Egypt, the people fell under God's judgment. None of the grown men except Caleb and Joshua, who had counseled trust in God, were allowed to enter Canaan. They were condemned to remain in the wilderness until they died. (See Numbers 14:1-38.)

Referring to these unfortunate events of his people's past, the psalmist warned those of his day against following the example of their fathers. He admonished them to obey God in order to escape similar judgment. The Hebrews writer referred to the words of the psalmist in delivering the same message to his readers. (1) He earnestly warned them against unfaithfulness to Christ. This unfaithfulness is characterized by the "evil heart of unbelief" and must be considered apostasy from God. It matters not whether it were an outright rejection of God or a return to Judaism after they had personally experienced the blessings of the gospel. (2) They were also exhorted to encourage each other to put their trust in God and respond to His Word while they had time and opportunity, in order to prevent their becoming attached to the deceptive and sinful character of this world. (3) Victory in

Christ belongs to those who are willing to preserve their confidence in Him and His promises. This admonition is a recurrent theme of the letter.

Loss of confidence in God, which persisted for forty years, kept Israel from entering Canaan. For God to command is for Him to imply that He will help one obey. After His people had experienced the exodus from Egypt and all His miraculous provisions in the wilderness, as well as the great experiences they had at Sinai, they universally rejected God's Word and were likewise rejected by Him. Disobedience is practically synonymous with unbelief, and God cannot allow it. We need to be constantly on guard in order that, having been redeemed and having enjoyed the blessings of salvation and the presence of God's Spirit in our lives, we do not lose our promise because of this basic sin of Israel—refusal to trust in God.

The parallel that the Hebrew letter drew between Israel and the church is by no means limited to this book. In 1 Corinthians 10, Paul compared the liberation of the Jews from Egypt and their failure in the wilderness journey with the salvation of believers in Christ and their need to persevere and overcome in the face of temptations and trials. "So, if you think you are standing firm, be careful that you don't fall!" (1 Corinthians 10:12).

The Rest Promised by God Is Still Available (4:1-10)

The author of Hebrews spent most of chapter 3 explaining that Israel under Moses failed to enter the rest offered in the promised land because of lack of faith in God. He warned his readers that the fatal consequence of loss of confidence in the redemptive Word of Christ is forfeiture of His promise to them. Developing this theme of God's promised rest, typified by Canaan in the Old Testament, the writer intended in this chapter to prove that this rest was still open, and to exhort his readers to enter into it.

He began this chapter at the very point where he left off in chapter 3. The cause of Israel's exclusion from the promised land was that they did not mix His promise with faith on their part. To refuse to obey is evidence enough that God's Word has not been received in trust and confidence.

"Faith comes from hearing the message, and the message is heard through the word of Christ" (Romans 10:17), if that word is received by the hearer. A faith thus generated is naturally followed by obedience on the part of the hearer and by the attendant blessing of God. Because the Jews under Moses acted as if God had never spoken, His Word gave them no benefit when they heard it. The writer of Hebrews urged his readers to be seriously concerned about a possible similar response on their part. He urged them to move forward lest they also would come short of God's promised rest. Loss of confidence in God holds the same danger for us that it did for Israel.

It is God's intention, and has been from the beginning, that believers enter into His promised rest, which He himself enjoys. Our Maker rested after His creation (Genesis 2:2) and assumes that men will share it when they finish their works. Because of unbelief, the Jews failed to enter into that rest. God's Word says that some will enjoy rest, but those to whom it was first promised did not enter in. Since God's Word cannot be broken, that rest is still open to all who will respond in faith.

The vital idea that the Hebrews writer conveyed is that the real promised rest of God was never intended to be Canaan. Of course, the Jews felt that they had already attained God's rest when they occupied the promised land under Joshua. The writer of this letter persuasively quotes from Psalm 95:7, 8, in which the psalmist, writing centuries after Joshua, said that "today" God's rest is available to those who will not harden their hearts to God's voice. If they had received under Joshua all that God had promised, why should David have been saying years later that it was still to be received?

The question that next arises is, what is the "Sabbath-rest" (used only here in Biblical Greek) that "remains...for the people of God" (Hebrews 4:9)? It has both a present and future reality. Canaan was, for the Jews, the end of their wandering. There is a very real sense in which it was a type, an unreal shadow, of the unbroken fellowship with good available to His people through faith in Jesus Christ. Did not our Lord say, "Come to me, all you who are weary and burdened, and I will give you rest" (Matthew 11:28)?

At the same time, one cannot help believing that the Hebrews writer had the final rest of God's people in mind. The believers' rest will not be complete until they reach that home where "they will rest from their labor, for their deeds will follow them" (Revelation 14:13). Heaven, although surely not a place of inactivity, will be free from the fatigue, exhaustion, weariness, and all of the toils, frustrations, and cares of this world.

Only the Obedient Enter That Rest (4:11-13)

The author of Hebrews exhorted his people to take God's Word seriously and press forward in order to enter into His rest. There was no room for a careless, frivolous approach or a defeatist attitude. Enjoying the rest of God requires earnest desire and determined effort.

To impress upon his readers the truth and certainty of the Word of God, which they must heed, he described it as "living and active," and "sharper than any double-edged sword." It goes into every part of the physical life, mental life, and spiritual life, perceiving even the thoughts and designs of one's mind. This brings to mind the picture of Jesus in Revelation 1:16 as the one out of whose mouth proceeded "a sharp double-edged sword," and Paul's description of the Word of God as the "sword of the Spirit" (Ephesians 6:17). It can probe even to the deepest level of human life.

The truth of God's Word is not blunted in any way, but lays all man's secrets open before his Maker's eyes. There is no area of one's life that is not clearly known to God through His Word. As the Lord said to Samuel at the time when the humble and lowly David—instead of one of his impressive-appearing brothers—was anointed to be king over Israel, "Man looks at the outward appearance, but the Lord looks at the heart" (1 Samuel 16:7). Nothing is hid from the penetrating observation of God, before whom we will give our account.

Since nothing escapes the observation of God, we cannot hope to achieve His promised rest on any other terms than His terms. There is no way but His way. Sincere obedient effort on man's part is necessary to reach God's promised rest.

Lessons From Chapter Three

Faith or Folly?

There are only two options open to us. We think we have many options, that we stand at the hub of a wheel and the opportunities, like spokes, reach out in many directions. We do have many options professionally. We do have many options when it comes to education. We do have many options regarding our place of residence. We do have many romantic, social, and recreational options. But spiritually, there are only two options. Either we doubt or we believe. We decide on the basis of the evidence; but it is also important to know the consequences. Fortunately, the consequences of our choices can be known in advance. There are many examples from Scripture and from life.

The Folly of Doubt

Israel is our example here. Doubt kept Israel in the desert. Had they not doubted, they could have gone directly from Egypt to Canaan, from slavery to the freedom of the Promised Land, from the banks of the Nile to the banks of the Jordan. But doubt kept them in the desert. It is not hard to see that doubt keeps us in a spiritual desert. It keeps us in a desert where showers of blessings do not come, where the sweet flowers of faith cannot grow.

Doubt kept Israel in the doldrums. Originally, the doldrums referred to a belt near the equator where the winds seldom blew and where sailing ships were becalmed. It has come to mean inactivity, stagnation, boredom. Israel spent forty years in the monotony of the wilderness where the landscape hardly changed, where the diet of manna never changed, and where every day was just like every other day. Men sin, sometimes, because they are bored and they think sin offers excitement. What they do not know is that one soon tires of a single sin and looks for excitement in another and then in another and then in another. Faith brings a vibrancy to life, but doubt is boring and monotonous. Doubt kept Israel out of the promised land.

Today anyone who can prove Jewish ancestry can emigrate to Israel. Then, they thought that just being a Jew got them to the land of promise. No. It was faith that made possible their entering. As long as they lacked faith, all their ancestry did them no good. Doubt still keeps people from the promised land. That land of better promises across another Jordan is reserved for those who truly believe.

The Personal Folly of Doubt

What happened to Israel collectively can happen to any one individually. What was for them a national problem can be for us a personal problem. Farther along in the book of Hebrews, in chapter 11, there is a roll call of the faithful. The Bible gives no roll call of the doubtful.

Still, one could be compiled. It is possible to look at that list and see for every believer his counterpart in a great disbeliever. For Abel, who shows his reverence by sacrificing his best, there is a Cain, who shows his contempt by his casualness. For every Noah, who heeds the warnings of God, there are a thousand who ignore them. For every Abraham, who trusts in the promises, there is always a Lot, who chooses the world's promises instead. For every Jacob, who cherishes his heritage, there is an Esau, who spurns them. For every Moses, whose faith makes him choose affliction, there is a Pharaoh, whose doubt makes him choose affluence. For every Joseph of forgiveness, there is a Judah of vengeance. For every Barak, who believes and obeys there is a Baalim, who doubts and disobeys. For every Jephthah, who keeps his vows, there is a Jeroboam, who forgets his vows. For every Daniel, who dares, there is a Diotrephes, who loves the world. For every faithful Samuel, there is an ill-fated Saul. For every prophet, a prodigal; for every doer, a doubter; for every believer, an unbeliever.

The Fruit of Faith

Four examples are held up for us in Hebrews 3 and in Psalm 95, which is quoted here. Moses is our example. Faith gave him courage—courage to go again into Egypt from which he had once fled. It gave him courage to stand before Pharaoh—a shepherd in his homespun robes before the wealthiest and most powerful man on earth. It gave him courage to demand Israel's freedom, courage to bring the plagues, and courage to lead the exodus.

Faith gave him confidence. Through forty years in the wilderness, he kept believing that God was leading and sustaining. He never doubted that the manna would fall, the water spring forth, or the day of inheritance arrive. Faith gave him character. Read the last chapter of Deuteronomy and see what the Bible says about the character of Moses.

What did faith do for Joshua, the second example? It gave him courage when he was one of the spies sent into Canaan. It gave him confidence when Jericho was attacked. It gave him character. Jesus bears the name of Joshua. What a compliment!

What did faith do for Caleb, companion of Joshua when the twelve spies went in? It gave him courage. Others called the Canaanites giants, but Caleb said, "We can certainly do it" (Numbers 13:30). It gave him confidence. He was eighty-five when the land was divided, but he said to Joshua, "Give me this hill country." He selected for himself the most difficult terrain, where the enemy was most entrenched. "Here I am," he said, "as strong today as the day Moses sent me out" (Joshua 14:6-15). It gave him character. Six times the Bible says that Caleb "followed the Lord wholeheartedly."

The best example is Jesus. Always, the best example is Jesus! He is an example in courage. He "resolutely set out for Jerusalem" when He knew that His enemies would kill Him there (Luke 9:51). He is our example in confidence. At the grave of Lazarus, He said, "I knew that you always hear me" (John 11:42). Perhaps the best of us cannot say that. Surely for us all there are times when it seems God isn't listening and when our prayers seem to be ineffective. Jesus could say, "I knew that you always hear me." Jesus is our example in character, for He "committed no sin, and no deceit was found in His mouth" (1 Peter 2:22). Faith will do all that for you. It will give you courage and confidence and character.

Faith-full and Faithful

English is a strange language. You would think that full of faith and faithful would be the same thing. They are not. They are related, but they are not the same thing. It is not those full of faith who are faithful; but faithfulness is a result of the fullness of faith. To be faithful is to be loyal, dependable, and true to one's commitments. To be full of faith is to have faith, but to be faithful is to keep the faith. It is to be true to the trust placed in us by others—and by God. Everybody adores the faithful, the people who will never betray a trust and never fail to keep faith with a commitment. Whenever we have not been faithful, it is because some doubt, however momentary or tentative, has crept in. Whenever we have been loyal and faithful, it is because doubt has been evicted by confident trust.

Part Two:

The Preeminence of Christ's High Priesthood

CHAPTER FOUR

Qualifications as High Priest

Hebrews 4:14-5:10

The Encouragement of Christ to Draw Near (4:14-16)

The writer of Hebrews encouraged his readers throughout this book to persevere in their trust and obedience to God. Here he reminded them that they had an added incentive to draw near to God in the powerful and sympathetic mediation of their high priest, Jesus, who was tempted in all respects according to His likeness to man. The Lord is able to understand man in his trials and temptations as no other one could ever do, because all others are limited by their own experiences. This is not true of Christ. His temptation went beyond that of anyone who ever lived.

In answer to those who reject the idea that Jesus could have sinned, as if the mere possibility would have obscured His divinity, we look to Hebrews. Unless Jesus was genuinely tempted, the writer's description of Jesus' sympathetic awareness of our condition is without actual foundation in fact. There is no indication in this chapter, or any other part of the letter, that Jesus was placed in any favorable position over other men in the trials He faced. He was certainly not beyond the reach of Satan's seducing power.

Some believers also shy away from the idea of our Lord's absolute temptation because they equate it with filth and base sin. Also, there are always the temptations for us that spring from our sins. How could Jesus ever be tempted to participate in some of the activities that the minds of men have produced? Of course, Jesus was not tempted to do or think many of the things that people often experience; but that mere fact does not rob Him of His capacity to sympathize. Because of His higher position and transcending power, His temptations would have been greater than those of any other being. On the high level on which Jesus lived, Satan tested Him to the fullest. Jesus' compassion is perfect because His temptation was complete. At the same time, Jesus is able to help us because He did not yield to temptation. Since He lived the perfectly sinless life, He is able to extend grace and mercy. Moreover, having overcome even to death, He ascended into Heaven and passed into the presence of God himself to intercede for us. Through His triumphant victory over the sins that plague us, we are encouraged to approach God through Him and receive the forgiveness and help that we need.

Once a year, on the Day of Atonement, the Jewish high priest entered the Holy of Holies to come before the presence of God. There, at the mercy seat, the high priest interceded for the people. Only through Jesus, however, was the way opened for man himself to approach God in such a clear, definite way. No other religious system has ever had this freedom, not even Judaism. Therefore, we are urged to draw near boldly to our Father through Jesus Christ, our high priest, with a confidence and assurance based on His complete understanding and His wonderful power to help.

Qualifications of a High Priest (5:1-4)

At the end of chapter 4, the author of Hebrews referred to the high priesthood of Christ, by which we can approach God and find the help we need to remain faithful to Him. The writer continued in chapter 5 to discuss this theme, which is probably the most important single subject of his book. The rest of the New Testament focuses attention on the facts of the gospel, the thirty-three-year ministry of our Lord and His promised return. The writer of Hebrews, on the other hand, placed special emphasis on the high priesthood of Jesus, His work of the past two thousand years, and His present ministry. He dealt in this section of the letter with the qualifications of a high priest and the manner in which our Lord so marvelously fulfills them.

First, a high priest had to be one of the people so that he could bear with the sins of their weakness. No one can adequately represent others if he has not had the experience necessary to understand and sympathize with their problems and predicaments. It is for this reason that candidates running for representative office generally make much of their status as veterans, property holders, parents of children in school, taxpayers, and so forth.

That the Aaronic order of priests shared in the weaknesses of those whom they represented is nowhere more clearly exemplified than in the sin of their father. Aaron, shortly before he began his official duties, participated in the shameful episode of the molding and worshiping of the golden calf (Exodus 32). Hebrews reminds us that because of this kinship of "weakness" between priest and people, the making of propitiation for the sins of the people had to await an offering for those of the high priest himself. On the Day of Atonement, therefore, he would offer a bull "for himself, and for his household" before he killed the goat and made atonement for Israel (Leviticus 16).

Also necessary to acceptable high-priestly function was divine selection. No man appoints himself in matters pertaining to God. Our Father reserved to himself the choice of those who would move between Him and the people as the mediator to offer propitiation for their sins. Anyone who reads Exodus, Leviticus, and Numbers will certainly notice the many references to God's personal choice of Aaron and his sons as priests. (For example, see Exodus 28:1.) One of the most disgraceful events in Israel's history involved the foolish attempt of Korah, Dathan, and Abiram to challenge the priestly position of Aaron and his sons and assume it for themselves. For this presumption on their part, they and their families were consumed under the terrible judgment of God (Numbers 16).

Jesus Qualifies Perfectly (5:5-10)

To demonstrate that Jesus received divine and perpetual appointment by His Father to His high-priestly ministry, the writer of Hebrews first appealed to Psalm 2:7, to which he had already referred in 1:5 in substantiating Jesus' divine sonship. Then he quoted Psalm 110:4 in introducing the subject of Jesus' succession to the order of Melchizedek, the ancient king of Salem and "priest of God Most High" (Genesis 14:18). Although it was merely mentioned in this chapter in order to show the divine selection of Jesus to His high-priestly office, the relationship between Christ and Melchizedek and its meaning and significance would be discussed later in chapter 7. There is much additional Scripture to illustrate for the believer that Jesus did not glorify himself but was sent of His Father to fulfill divine mission and purpose. (See John 5:30; 6:38, and other passages in John.)

Not only was our Lord divinely called to His priestly ministry; He also came from among the people. Already in chapter 2, the writer explained why it was necessary that Jesus become a man. In that same context was mentioned the humanity of Jesus, which equipped Him to be "a merciful and faithful high priest" (2:17). In the present chapter, the earthly life of God's Son was mentioned to show that although Jesus lived sinlessly, through His sufferings, temptations, and death, He fully and completely identified himself with man.

Although there were perhaps many occasions in which he "offered up prayers and petitions with loud cries and tears," the most obvious such event in Jesus' life was His experience in Gethsemane. There, with a soul "overwhelmed with sorrow to the point of death" (Mark 14:34), He prayed that, if it were possible, His Father would remove the cup from Him. Continuing in His "anguish he prayed more earnestly, and his sweat was like great drops of blood falling to the ground" (Luke 22:44). God answered Jesus' prayer and gave Him strength to submit to His Father's will.

In saying that Jesus "learned obedience from what he suffered" (5:8), the writer was not suggesting that Jesus learned how to obey; He already knew that. He meant that, although Jesus was the Son of God, He learned from human experience what obedience meant, what it involved, and particularly the suffering that could result from it. In fact, preparation for His high-priestly ministry was completed in the suffering that He thus experienced. Through His successful endurance of that suffering, Jesus brought salvation to those who obey Him and was "designated by God to be high priest in the order of Melchizedek."

Lessons From Chapter Four

"Whereas" Always Leads to "Therefore"

If you have been in many assemblies that pass resolutions, you know that there are many paragraphs that begin with "Whereas," but only the final one begins with "Therefore." Charles L. Allen used to say that he never paid much attention to the "whereas," but he always took notice when they got to the "therefore." Hebrews 4:14 begins, "Therefore."

It is not that the "whereases" are not important. They are quite important. They are the foundation upon which the "therefores" rest. However, the "therefore" becomes the sharp point of the pencil that brings all to bear upon life and its deeds.

There was once a very popular show called "Truth or Consequences." If you didn't answer a question successfully, a buzzer sounded and you were told: "You didn't tell the truth; so you must pay the consequences." Then some practical joke was played on the contestant. We don't like to consider the consequences. Yet all our deeds have consequences; and some of them have eternal consequences.

Practical Theology

In colleges and seminaries, the courses that deal with methods of preaching or church administration are called "Practical Theology." But all theology does not seem practical. Yet Hebrews, the most theological book in the New Testament, certainly is also one of the most practical. The theology is about Christ. Who is He? He is the Son of God. Where is He? In the Heavens at the right hand of God. That's theology. *"Let us hold firmly"* (Hebrews 4:15). That's practical! If we are tempted to let go of our faith, we remember Who Jesus is! If we are tempted to deny our faith, we remember where Jesus is! His *person* and His *position* reassure us. We cannot give up what we believe! Persecution must not make us give it up. Temptation must not make us give it up. Discouragement must not make us give it up. Pain and suffering must not make us give it up. Disappointment must not make us give it up. The reason we must hold fast our profession is centered in Who Jesus is and where Jesus is!

Sometimes, though, the solving of one problem only produces another. Since Jesus is God's Son and at God's side, we must believe. But can we approach such a Christ? Is He so grand as to be unapproachable? We need to know not only Who and where He is, but how He is affected by us. The answer is that He is touched with the feeling of our infirmities!

The Greeks believed in a god unmoved by man's sufferings. A god so moved would not be god, they thought. For if he could be moved by man's plight, then he would not be all powerful or sovereign. That was faulty thinking. Because He shared our life, with its temptation and pain, we know He understands.

Now Christ did not have to come in the flesh to understand us. He is omniscient and has always understood us. He had to come in the flesh so that we would know that He understands us! There is something practical about this bit of theology, too.

Let Us Come Boldly

He is neither too high nor too mighty to hear our prayers and to help us. There are some grand examples of such boldness in the Bible. You see it in Jacob's wrestling with the angel (Genesis 32:24-32). You see it in Moses' pleading with God to forgive Israel (Exodus 32:31, 32). You see it in Jesus, too. Even on the cross, He believed God was still His Father Who heard and heeded His prayers.

The results of such boldness are mercy and grace. Mercy means we don't get the punishment we deserve. Grace means we do get the blessings we don't deserve. Mercy is being let off even when we deserve the sentence. Grace is being let back into the family even when we don't deserve it.

Then there is help in our time of need. Often, we do not fully understand the help we need. A minister once said he helped everyone who came to the church asking for help. Some he helped by giving them what they wanted and some he helped by refusing to give them what they wanted. Certainly, to have handed money to some of them would not really have helped them, though it would have been just what they wanted. So God always helps. He does not always give us what we want. He does not always do what we ask. But he always helps in time of need. Sometimes we do not understand His help, but we must trust His wisdom and love. The problem is we cannot always tell the difference between what we need and what we want. God can tell the difference.

What Christ knew by intellect He learned again through experience in His sufferings. In a different way, we, too, learn by suffering. In Thessalonica, Greece, stands the grand old St. Demetrius church. At one period, it was taken over by the Moslems. They turned it into a mosque. They plastered over the lovely Christian mosaics. It was a mosque for so long a time that people forgot the mosaics were ever there. Even after it had become a church again, no one remembered the earlier Christian art. Then the church caught fire. The fire caused the plaster to fall and the Christian mosaics reappeared. In a similar way, suffering may cause us to remember what we once knew and have forgotten. Suffering may teach us new truths, give us new insights. Suffering may reveal to us a hidden beauty that, otherwise, we would never see.

We also learn something from the suffering of Jesus. We must never forget that His suffering was real. The fact of His deity does not diminish the pain of his suffering. Hebrews 5:7 marks both Jesus' tears and His fears! He experiences life "in the raw." We learn something from His suffering. We learn the length of His patience, the depth of His love, the strength of His character.

CHAPTER FIVE

The Christian's Confidence in Christ

Hebrews 5:11-6:20

Description of Spiritual Immaturity (5:11-14)

The Hebrews writer was ready in Hebrews 5:11 to discuss the Melchizedek order and its relationship to Christ. But because it is such a difficult subject, he digressed from his main argument to comment on their spiritual immaturity and admonish them to grow up in Christ.

Far from being able to excuse themselves on the basis of the shortness of the time that had elapsed since their conversion, they had been Christians long enough to have been engaged in the instruction of others. Instead, they themselves still did not understand the elementary truths of God's revelation. Using the analogy of the dining table, the writer emphasized that their lack of development in Christ had resulted from failure to include in their spiritual diet the solid food of knowledge and experience in deeper truths of God's revelation. Progress in spiritual understanding, like growth in any other area of human existence, involves practice and experience. Quite simply stated, the exercise of one's spiritual faculties develops his spiritual perception. As we seek greater insights into the mysteries of faith, we have richer experiences in Christ; and as we have richer experiences in Christ, we receive greater insights into the mysteries of faith.

Warning Against Apostasy (6:1-8)

Perhaps this reasoning prompted the writer as he began chapter 6 to issue a call to his readers to move toward maturity in Christ. They needed to grow in order to understand the high priesthood of Christ, and instruction in His high priesthood may be the very thing that they needed to help them grow.

The author listed six foundational principles of Christian doctrine beyond which his readers needed to go if they were going to escape spiritual infancy and grow up.

1. The *repentance* he described may be from works of the flesh that produce death (Romans 6:23; Galatians 5:19-21), from works of men "dead in transgressions and sins" (Ephesians 2:1), or from works of the law, which cannot bring life.

2. *Faith* is the most basic part of one's redemptive relationship to God. "For it is by grace you have been saved, through faith—and this not from yourselves, it is the gift of God" (Ephesians 2:8). Although belief naturally leads to repentance, as in the case of the Jewish converts at Pentecost (Acts 2), true repentance conditions one to experience deep faith in God.

3. The use of the term *instruction about baptisms* (plural) by the writer of Hebrews has made it difficult to know precisely what he meant by this fundamental element of doctrine beyond which they needed to move. Some students of the letter suggest that he was referring to Christian immersion in water contrasted to the baptism of the Holy Spirit and fire (Matthew 3:11; Acts 1:5). Others believe that he was speaking of Christian baptism, John's baptism, and the many Jewish washings. Still others think that he was merely referring to the Jewish ceremonial washings (Mark 7:4; Hebrews 9:10) that were a part of what the readers left when they came to Christ.

4. The *laying on of hands* probably referred to the imparting of the special gifts of the Spirit by the apostles (Acts 6:6; 8:17; 19:6). It may also have been an allusion to the healing of the sick (Acts 9:17; 28:8) or the ordaining of men to service in the leadership of the church (Acts 6:6; 13:3; 1 Timothy 4:14; 5:22).

5. Not only was the *resurrection of the dead* central in the gospel message, as one can see in all the recorded sermons in Acts, but other basic teaching on the subject would have been necessary for Jewish converts, since the Pharisees and Sadducees were sharply divided over it (Matthew 22:23-32; 1 Corinthians 15:12-14; Mark 12:18-27; Acts 23:6-9).

6. In addition to being one of the recurrent themes of our Lord's teaching, the *eternal judgment* of God was one of those basic realities of which Jesus said the Holy Spirit would convict the world when He came (John 16:8, 11). (See Acts 17:31, 32 for the place of God's judgment in the fundamental gospel message of the apostles.)

Although confident that with God's help his readers could advance toward full growth in Christ, the writer did stop to warn them that failure to do so could result in the outright denial of Christ and one's relationship to Him. An understanding of merely the elementary doctrines of the faith was not sufficient to enable them to withstand the subtle pressures leading them toward the peril of apostasy.

The writer began his warning with a brief list of the blessings of life in Christ that one renounces when he turns his back on the Lord after experiencing salvation in Him. (1) There is the marvelous translation from darkness to light that only a child of God can know. (See 2 Corinthians 4:6; Ephesians 5:8; 1 Peter 2:9.) There is such a historically traditional relationship between enlightenment in Christ and baptism that many students of Hebrews believe the writer was referring to baptism at this point. (2) Suggested meanings for the "heavenly gift" that they had "tasted" range all the way from the grace of God, the Holy Spirit, and Christ himself, to eternal life and the Lord's Supper. Redemption in Christ would appear to be the most natural explanation. (3) One of God's greatest blessings is the indwelling presence of the Holy Spirit (described so beautifully in Romans 8) in the lives of His people. The temple of the body houses the very Spirit of God himself (1 Corinthians 6:19). (4) In Christ, one also personally experiences the fruit of God's Word in his own life, such as its faith-generating power (Romans 10:17) and its sanctifying influence (1 Timothy 4:5). (5) The "powers of the coming age" are generally considered to be the miraculous gifts displayed throughout the book of Acts and discussed in 1 Corinthians 12-14.

The writer continued by referring to one who willfully and deliberately repudiates Christ. This one has personally experienced all of the blessings and the redemptive power that God has released into this world through His Son. Now by his rejection, the willful one says that there is nothing to what God has done for him, nothing to what he has experienced in Christ. He makes repentance impossible for himself, probably because he will not seek it. In taking this step, he has reenacted the crucifixion of Christ in his own life and exposed his Lord to ridicule before the world.

It should be noted that the condition being described in this chapter is not simply postbaptismal sin or what is commonly called "backsliding." Some would suggest, however, that the indifference of backsliding could lead to deliberate and conscious falling away.

The obvious point that the author of Hebrews was making in this severe admonition is that failure to move toward spiritual maturity and bear fruit for God in one's life is a road that leads to apostasy. Those who do not go forward are likely to go back. God has made a great investment in us through Christ, and He expects a return. Rejection and ultimate destruction will be the lot of a Christian who fails to grow, just as it is with cultivated and planted ground that produces no harvest.

Vote of Confidence (6:9-12)

The severe warning of Hebrews 6:1-8 is followed by the writer's assertion of confidence in his readers' fidelity to Christ. He assured them that God remembered what they had done in serving their fellow Christians and would continue to bless them for it. He further encouraged them to disallow any tendency toward spiritual laziness or inactivity and to continue to persevere diligently in the assurance of their hope as they sought to imitate the great heroes of faith who had gone before them.

Hope Based on God's Promises (6:13-20)

The confidence of hope that Christians are to maintain is based on nothing less than the promises of God and the example of those who have already trusted in Him. These have proved His faithfulness to His promises. The writer selected Abraham as the classic example of one who believed God, persevered through faith in His promise, and experienced the fulfillment (at least in part) of that promise. The particular promise referred to in verse 14 is recorded in Genesis 22:16, 17, and was made following Abraham's near-offering up of his son Isaac. It was a repetition of God's pledge to bless Abraham and make of him a great nation. Of course, this promise would have its ultimate fulfillment in the coming of Christ into the world to save mankind.

The certainty of this promise made earlier in Genesis 12 rested on two firm and unalterable grounds: God's Word and the oath by which He affirmed it. Since men substantiate their words to each other with oaths, God condescended to man's level and confirmed His Word of promise with an oath. God's Word is always more than enough in itself. An oath carries the force of a legal guarantee. Using both would further reveal the unchangeableness of God's purpose and give man all the assurance it was possible to give. The oath is found in these words of Hebrews 6:14, literally translated, "Blessing I will bless," and, "Multiplying I will multiply." The emphasis and repetition of the words *bless* and *multiply* carry the force of absolute certainty. Since there was neither anyone nor anything greater than God by which He could swear, His oath was based on himself. No promise could ever be more binding.

Thus, the believer's hope, which springs from his confidence in God's promises, is the firm anchor for his soul. It gives security and stability to our spiritual lives. Moreover, because Jesus has gone before us through the curtain of the Holy of Holies into the very presence of God, our hope reaches through the curtain also, and through our confidence in Christ as our priest after the order of Melchizedek we too can enter into God's presence.

Lessons From Chapter Five

The hymn "The Solid Rock" by Edward Mote is an outline of this section of Hebrews.

My hope is built on nothing less
Than Jesus' blood and righteousness;
I dare not trust the sweetest frame,
But wholly lean on Jesus' name

His oath, His covenant, His blood
Support me in the 'whelming flood
When all around my soul gives way,
He then is all my hope and stay.

Oath, covenant, and blood are the themes of this lesson. If we look at them in reverse order, we see that our hope is secured by His blood, supported by His covenant, and confirmed by His oath.

The blood of Jesus is the theme of the first ten chapters of Hebrews. In fact, those ten chapters really have two points to make: "Jesus comes first" and "There is power in the blood." We recall the Jewish worship, with the blood of a lamb from the altar carried by the High Priest into the Most Holy Place. For us, Christ has a dual role: He is both the Lamb Who sheds the blood and the Priest Who carries the blood. He carries it up to Heaven, the Holiest of All. That establishes our hope.

Our hope is supported by a covenant. Through the Scriptures, God is a covenant-keeping God. He made covenants with Noah, Abraham, Moses, David, Israel as a nation, and with us! Once there was a group of Scots who bound themselves together because of both their faith and their patriotism; and they are known to history as the Covenanters. All Christians are covenanters. We are heirs of a covenant that God dictated and whose benefits we enjoy.

Our hope is confirmed by an oath. We use an oath in the courtroom, at the marriage altar, and when one joins the army or takes public office. We even hear it on the playground: "Cross my heart and hope to die!" If the oath is so much a part of the fabric of life, we are not surprised that God should use this means to reassure us. In an oath, one swears by something greater than himself. In the courtroom, it is on the Bible and "so help me God." On the playground ("cross my heart and hope to die") it is on one's very life. Always, one swears by something greater than himself. But since there is no other greater than God, He swore by himself.

Why did He do that? Why not just say as some do, "You'll have to take my word for it. I'll sign no paper. I'll take no oath. Just take my word for it." Why didn't God do that? The answer is here in chapter 6, verses 17 and 18:

> Because God wanted to make the unchanging nature of his purpose very clear to the heirs of what was promised, he confirmed it with an oath. God did this so that, by two unchangeable things in which it is impossible for God to lie, we who have fled to take hold of the hope offered to us may be greatly encouraged.

He wanted to make it completely clear. He wanted to make it absolutely certain.

The fruits of hope are here. One is purity. Hebrews 6 hints at it. First John 3:3 spells it out: "Everyone who has this hope in him purifies himself." Why does hope make men pure? Because he who has hope doesn't have to grasp today, filling every moment with pleasure and wringing every drop of happiness out of every day. He can wait. He has a future that will get brighter and brighter. He doesn't need to grasp today. He doesn't want to lose tomorrow. That's why hope makes men pure.

Hope gives us patience. We speak of the patience of Job; but this Scripture speaks of the patience of Abraham. God promised a son, but the months stretched into years and the years into decades; and Abraham was still childless. God promised a land; yet all Abraham owned was a cemetery lot. If that is all you own, don't worry. Just identify with Abraham. But Abraham patiently waited for God to fulfill His promise.

Surely, our hope gives us a sense of perspective. Visitors to the Kennedy Space Center are a little disappointed at first at the Vehicle Assembly Building. Touted as the largest building in the world, it does not seem too impressive at first glance. One approaches it over the flat scrub of Merritt Island. There are no structures nearby for a comparison. There is nothing by which the eye can measure. Without a perspective, it seems quite ordinary. Then one goes inside. There is a man on a scaffold, appearing no bigger than a fly. There are the clouds that form at the top, actually making it rain *inside* the building. Then, having acquired his perspective, the visitor is able to grasp its immensity. So hope gives us a sense of perspective. We can see what is large in life and what is little in life. We can tell what is important and what is insignificant.

There is a natural hope and a spiritual hope. There is a Christian hope and a human hope. One is a very large idea that joins faith and love as the three great aspects of Christianity. It is certain, positive, and virile. The other is an uncertain and wistful optimism, a temporary cheerfulness that probably things are going to work out somehow.

It is of this second hope that Benjamin Franklin said, "He who lives on hope will die fasting." Other descriptions of this hope are: "Hope is like snow in the desert" (Omar Khayyam). "Hope is a quivering, nervous creature trying to be bright and cheerful but, alas, frequently sick, abed with nervous prostration and heart failure" (author unknown).

How different is the Biblical hope. "For in this hope we were saved." (Romans 8:24). "And now these three remain: faith *hope* and love" (1 Corinthians 13:13). "Hope does not disappoint us" (Romans 5:5). "We have this hope as an anchor for the soul" (Hebrews 6:19).

We need an anchor for the storms of life. They *will* come. We need an anchor for the tides of life, lest the currents of the world sweep us away. We need an anchor for the harbor of life, that we may at last dock in a peaceful haven. We need an anchor so badly that we seize on everything that seems like a possible anchor.

Some see education as an anchor, but it was the most educated nation on earth that gave birth to the Nazi atrocities. Some see health as an anchor, but much of the work in the world is done by people who don't feel like doing it. Some see wealth as an anchor. That turns out like the ship, "Marine Electric." Early in 1983, the ship sunk off the Virginia coast, costing the lives of thirty-one sailors. The reason? The ship's eight-ton anchor came loose. It battered the hull of the ship till she went down. The ship was destroyed by its own anchor. If wealth is your anchor, that may well be your experience. Some see friends as their anchor—family, career, pleasure—but all will finally fail.

Our hope in Christ is the only sure anchor for the soul. At the Peabody Maritime Museum in Salem, Massachusetts, there is a two-ton anchor on display. It has been twisted by the sea. So great is the force of the waves that they twisted that two-ton anchor! "Will your anchor hold in the storms of life?"

CHAPTER SIX

Superior to Jewish Order

Hebrews 7:1-28

Characteristics of the Melchizedek Priesthood (7:1-3)

In mentioning the high priesthood of Christ after the order of Melchizedek (6:20), the author of Hebrews returned to the theme that he had temporarily left in 5:10. He was here ready to deal with that subject thoroughly and to explain its implications to the lives of believers.

The major theme of this book is the preeminence of Christianity over Judaism. Any claim to such preeminence, however, must rest on a higher priesthood, since the whole Old Testament law and system of sacrifices were founded on the Levitical priesthood. Following that line of reasoning, the Hebrews writer asserted that the priesthood of Jesus was greater than the Levitical priesthood because it was after the order of Melchizedek. To substantiate that contention, he needed to prove that the order of Melchizedek was superior to that of Aaron.

His description of Melchizedek was obviously based on the account in Genesis 14 of Abraham's return from victory over Kedorlaomer and the kings that were with him. These kings had plundered Sodom and the surrounding cities. Abraham, the father of the Jews, paid tithes to the king of Salem (probably old Jerusalem), "priest of God Most High," and was in turn blessed by him.

In addition to his reference to the tithes and blessing, the writer briefly noted four characteristics of Melchizedek and his priesthood: (1) The name, Melchizedek, means "king of righteousness." His title, "king of Salem," literally means "king of peace." Jesus lived a righteous life when He was here on earth. He came to bring peace. Just as Melchizedek was a royal priest, even so Jesus is both king and priest. (2) Melchizedek had neither father nor mother, neither beginning nor end. Many believe that this description implies that there is no. account of his genealogy. His ancestry is unrecorded and unknown. Some suggest that he actually had no father or mother, that he was a supernatural being who was miraculously sent by God. Still others more specifically consider him to have been an earthly manifestation of Jesus Christ in the Old Testament. (3) He was "like the Son of God." Again opinions would differ over whether this description means that he was a type of Christ or a manifestation of Christ himself. (4) His priesthood lasts forever. There is no record of either its beginning or its end.

The Superiority of the Melchizedek Order (7:4-10)

With verse 4, the writer began the development of his brief but logical proof for the superiority of Melchizedek over the Jewish priests. His case rests on three basic ideas: (1) The Levitical priests received tithes of their brothers, while the greatness of Melchize-dek is implicit in his receiving tithes of Abraham, the father of both the priests and the people who tithed. (2) Since the greater always blesses the lesser, Melchizedek must be higher than the Levites, for he blessed the father of all of them. (3) Whereas the Levitical priests died and passed on their ministries to their descendants, there is no record that Melchizedek died. His was not a hereditary priesthood, but an eternal one.

To further his argument, the writer added the suggestion that, in a certain sense, Levi himself could be considered to have paid tithes to Melchizedek, since he was figuratively present in his grandfather Abraham through ancestry and descent.

The Need for a Greater High Priesthood (7:11-19)

The superiority of the Melchizedek order to which Christ belonged carried with it two logical and profound implications: (1) A new order and change of priesthood means that the old Aaronic order was impermanent and imperfect. (2) Since the Old Testament law was conditioned on the old priesthood, a change of priesthood inevitably brought about a change in the law.

The writer affirmed that the extreme nature of the change that occurred was indicated by the fact that the new high priest, Jesus, was not even a Levite. He came from the tribe of Judah and was of the royal lineage of David. The law of Moses gave no indication that priestly duties were to be performed by any member of that tribe.

The author of Hebrews further elaborated on the impermanence of the Levitical priesthood by emphasizing that it rested on a "regulation as to … ancestry." This statement could mean that since it was established with the giving of the law on Mt. Sinai, it began in time and was subject to end in time. Another possible explanation is that it was based on ritual, ceremonial purity, observation of rules, offering of the animal sacrifices, and the family descent of the priests. It was concerned with physical worth, not a man's character or ability.

Christ, on the other hand, was declared to be "a priest forever" (Psalm 110:4). His priesthood rests on the "power of an indestructible life." It depends on His character, His personality, His very being. Like Melchizedek, Jesus had neither "beginning nor end." (See Micah 5:2; John 1:1.)

Perhaps the greatest imperfection and inadequacy of the legal and priestly system of the Old Testament lay in the fact that it failed to provide the means for drawing near to God. In one sense, the people were separated from God by a class of people designated as priests.

Christ Is the Greater High Priest (7:20-28)

In the remainder of chapter 7, the Hebrews writer gave additional proof for the superiority of the priesthood of Christ. Further employing the prophecy of Psalm 110:4 concerning the Melchizedek order, the writer pointed out that God confirmed our Lord's priesthood through an oath in contrast to that of the Levitical order, which was given without an oath. Thus, the unalterable and eternal nature of the priesthood of Jesus was substantiated by God's own oath.

Still another part of the Old Testament system affected by Christ's higher priesthood was God's covenant with the Jews. Since His covenant relationship with them was also based on the legal-priestly order established at Sinai, a change in that order would carry with it a change in the covenant. So Christ, the greater high priest, became the guarantor of a better covenant.

Ample signs of the impermanence of the Levitical order under the Old Covenant were seen in the constant change of priests resulting from their removal by death. Under the old, there were many in number; the priesthood passed from one to another. Under the new, there is only one, and He lives forever.

Because He never dies, and His priesthood is eternal and unchangeable, Christ is able to save completely, now and for all time, those who come to Him. His intercession for His people is constant and continual. Under the Old Testament system, the priests interceded for the people through sacrifices at certain times, and the high priest on the Day of Atonement once each year. But the intercession of our high priest, Jesus, is not intermittent or spasmodic. There is not a moment in which He is not interceding for those who abide in Him.

The complete efficacy of Jesus' saving intercession rests on His perfect life. Unlike the Levitical priests, who were weak and had to offer sacrifices for their own sins before they could intercede for the people, Christ was holy, sinless, and without stain or blemish. God has now removed Jesus from the realm of sinners and elevated Him above the heavens. Thus, His sacrifice of himself once, the perfect final sacrifice, and His divine oath-bound appointment as high priest by His Father make Jesus fully qualified to serve in the Heavenly sanctuary. He is able to save perfectly and completely those who approach God through Him.

Lessons From Chapter Six

A Man Who Stood Taller

Robert Wadlow was the world's tallest man. He was born in Alton, Illinois, in 1918. When he died in 1940 in Michigan, he was 8 feet, 11.1 inches tall. Some people, however, stand tall in spiritual, not physical, dimensions. Abraham stood tall in Hebrew history. In this lesson we meet a man who stood taller—Melchizedek; and we consider one who stood taller still—Jesus.

Solving an Ancient Mystery

When God called Abraham to leave pagan Ur for pagan Canaan, Abraham did not expect to find any one there who worshiped God. To his surprise, there was a God-fearing man in Canaan. He was a man of considerable stature. He was both a priest and a king. He was not a priest of Astarte. He was not a priest of Baal. He was not a priest of any of the Canaanite idols. he was a priest of Jehovah. How did he learn about God? Who led him to such faith? We do not know, of course. But behind every known there is an unknown. Name any famous preacher, and you will find that a far less-famous preacher, or perhaps an unknown Sunday-school teacher, provided the spiritual guidance and inspiration that was needed. Just think of your own life. Who influenced you? There's a more important question. Whom are you influencing?

Bread and Blessing

Read the account of Melchizedek in Genesis. Abraham has returned from a military campaign. Evil marauding kings had been sweeping across the land burning, pillaging, robbing, and killing. They had kidnapped Abraham's nephew, Lot. Abraham mustered an army, set out in pursuit of them, and rescued Lot. He is returning from this victory when he comes to Salem (Jerusalem) and meets Melchizedek. Bread and wine are brought and Melchizedek blesses Abraham. Bread and wine and blessing suggest

Communion. And at Communion, we are, like Abraham, celebrating a victory.

It is not just commemoration at Communion—it is also celebration. We not only celebrate Christ's victory at Calvary, but our own spiritual victories, too. Never is there a Sunday but what we can look back upon some spiritual victory: some temptation resisted, some weakness overcome, some burden borne, or some task done.

In addition, Abraham and Melchizedek were cementing a friendship. It was the custom of the East that to eat with a man meant that you were friends and bound to defend one another. Is not Communion also cementing a friendship? Is it not the time when we remember the Friend we have in Jesus and pledge ourselves anew to Him? And in both events, the common symbolizes the uncommon. What is so common as bread and wine? What is so uncommon as loyalty and sacrifice?

Tithes and Offerings

A minister once said that he had practiced tithing all his life but had not preached it in the early years of his ministry. For him, it wasn't necessary to say, "Practice what you preach," but, "Preach what you practice." He said that this very passage caused him to preach tithing. Tithing is honoring one who is greater! That's the reason Abraham gave tithes to Melchizedek and not the other way around. Surely, Christ, our High Priest, is greater than Melchizedek. Does He deserve less? And, like Communion, giving is a way of celebrating victory!

Purity and Peace

Salem means "peace" and Melchizedek means "righteousness." Do you think the man's name affected his life? If your name were Joy, would you feel an obligation to be extra cheerful? If your name were Grace, would it affect your personality? Is it a mistake that nobody is named Prudence any more? Added to his name "righteousness" is his title "king of peace." Before Jesus ever came to be our eternal Prince of Peace, this man was called the King of Peace. You must not miss the order in which the terms come. It is not peace first and then righteousness. It is righteousness first and then peace. If you have no peace in your heart, it may be because you have not yet made peace with God! Purity first, then peace; and never the other way around.

Priest and King

Usually the offices were separate, priest and king. There are a few exceptions in history. Egypt at one period had a line of priest-kings. In South America, there was a period when priest-kings ruled. European history takes note of a time when the Pope at Rome had temporal and spiritual power, when he crowned the kings of Europe. Once he kept the emperor standing out in the cold for three days before he let the man in and they were reconciled. Usually, however, priest and king have been separate offices. It is so in the Bible, with only two exceptions—Melchizedek and Christ. For Christ is both priest and king. He also carried a third responsibility: He is Prophet, Priest, and King!

In Bemidji, Minnesota, you may see a statue of Paul Bunyan—not life-size, of course! For Paul Bunyan was the mythical giant of Western America. He dragged his pick behind him and made the Grand Canyon! He combed his beard with a pine tree! A lake was used to hold the batter for his pancakes, and a steamboat mixed the batter! Legends, of course! Neither Melchizedek nor Jesus were legendary figures; but they were Bunyanesque figures. They seem almost larger than life. But Jesus towers above even Melchizedek as King of Kings and Lord of Lords.

That places a certain demand upon us. It was enough that Abraham make a courtesy call on Melchizedek, stop for a few moments, and go on his way. But that will not do with Jesus. We cannot merely pay Him a courtesy call on Sunday and go our way. We cannot simply give Him a few moments. We must give Him our lives. A minister was counseling a couple about to be married. "I'm going to give you a life sentence," he said. The young man said, "Well, we'd hoped to be together forever, but I guess we'll have to settle for just one lifetime." The best part of the bargain is that when we give Jesus our lifetime, He gives us His eternity.

Part Three:

The Preeminence of the New Covenant

CHAPTER SEVEN

Christ the Mediator

Hebrews 8:1-13

The True Tabernacle (8:1-5)

The author of Hebrews rather elaborately proved in chapter 7 that in contrast to the Levitical priests, Christ is fully qualified to serve as a greater and permanent high priest. In chapter 8, he entered into a lengthy discussion (running through 10:18) of the priestly ministry that our Lord fulfills and its relationship to the covenant, tabernacle, and sacrifice of the Jewish system.

Although he would treat the sanctuary in which Christ serves and the sacrifice that He offers more thoroughly in chapters 9 and 10, the writer introduced them in the early verses of chapter 8. The logic of Hebrews is that where there is a high priest, there must also be a sanctuary; and where there is a sanctuary, there will be sacrifices and other priestly activities performed. The place where Jesus discharges His priestly service is the Heavenly tabernacle.

As was already mentioned in chapter 7, Jesus did not belong to the priestly tribe while He lived on earth and did not minister in the temple. He went to the temple several times for Jewish feasts, to worship, and to teach. On two occasions He went to "purify" it of sacrilegious practices. He did not, however, frequent the court of priests, offer sacrifices in the temple proper, or serve in any other priestly capacity. In fact, Jesus was attacked by the priests for His teaching.

Even the Old Testament background for the building of the tabernacle gave clear indications that it was only a shadow, an imitation of the Heavenly prototype. Ezekiel 40-45 furnishes an interesting study for a Bible student who wishes to explore further the idea of the Heavenly temple. Although one does not have to infer at all from the words of the Hebrews writer that the earthly tabernacle of the Jews was a literal replica of the one in Heaven, there is no questioning his suggestion that the Jewish one was an unreal imitation of the Heavenly archetype.

In mentioning this idea of the true spiritual tabernacle in Heaven, the writer introduced a concept that is vital to an understanding of this book. The contrast between the realm of the spirit and that of the physical is the difference between reality and appearance. Accordingly, Paul wrote to the Corinthians, "For what is seen is temporary, but what is unseen is eternal" (2

Corinthians 4:18). The Heavenly sphere of the spirit, not the earthly world of the flesh, constitutes eternal reality.

While Jesus gave no indication in His earthly ministry of being a priest, it was toward the end of His ministry that He offered the sacrifice that paved the way for His entrance into the Heavenly sanctuary as our great high priest. The giving of himself in death on Calvary as a sacrifice for the redemption of mankind was the first priestly function that Jesus performed.

(At this point, we notice that the discussion has returned to the theme that makes Hebrews' most significant and unique contribution to our understanding and appreciation of the total ministry of Jesus Christ. [See the notes on Hebrews 5:1-4, above.] The author of this book was primarily concerned with the present ministry of Jesus instead of His earthly ministry of A.D. 26-30.)

Far from conveying any idea that the place where Christ serves is inferior to the earthly tabernacle of the Jews, the Hebrews writer affirmed that the Jewish sanctuary was only a copy of the of the true tabernacle in Heaven. He was eager to remind his readers that Moses was instructed to construct the tabernacle according to the pattern that he was shown in the mountain. (See Exodus 25:40.)

The Better Covenant (8:6-13)

The preeminence of Christ's high-priestly ministry is not only authenticated by the superior tabernacle in Heaven in which He serves, but also by the new and better covenant on which it rests and of which He is the mediator. The writer had already implied the higher origin of the New Covenant in his discussion of the superiority of Christ to Moses, through whose mediating agency the Old Covenant of the Jews was delivered (Galatians 3:19). Moreover, the very fact that the Old Covenant had been replaced by the New was evidence enough that the Old was imperfect and inadequate and that the New is a better covenant based on better promises. The Hebrews writer quoted Jeremiah 31:31-34, a passage in which the prophet predicted that God would make a New Covenant with His people and described the better promises on which it would be established. Far from being a novel and strange idea, the concept of the New Covenant had been prophesied hundreds of years before Christ.

After God had delivered the Hebrews from Egyptian bondage, He established a peculiar relationship with them at Sinai, one that He shared with no other people. He promised to be their God and to bless them. They in turn pledged themselves to serve and obey Him. The basis of this unique relationship was the Old Covenant, and the terms of the Jews' allegiance to it were the Ten Commandments and the law derived from them. From the time that God made His covenant with Israel until the days of Jeremiah, their history had been one long series of failures to keep their part of the covenant. Finally, the judgment of God fell, the city of Jerusalem was destroyed, and most of the people were carried into exile in Babylon.

It was in this context that Jeremiah prophesied the New Covenant, to which the Hebrews writer referred in this chapter. Because Israel had broken the Old Covenant by their repeated transgressions, God determined to make a new and different one. The significance and importance of the divine origin and author-ship of the New Covenant was emphasized by the fact that three times within the prophecy, phrases are introduced by "This is what the Lord says."

First, the terms of the New Covenant are not written on tablets of stone, but on the warm flesh of the heart. The Old Covenant could restrain men only outwardly. It failed to provide them the power to keep God's Word and resist evil because "it was weakened by the sinful nature" (Romans 8:3). In contrast to this, the motivating force of the New Covenant is a changed man, a new nature. Under it, men receive a new heart and are freed from the bondage of sin. (See Romans 6.) A basic feature of man's relationship to God through the New Covenant is that allegiance and obedience to Him spring from the desire of the Holy Spirit instead of legal prohibition. Morality and spirituality are prompted from within, not from without.

Certainly implied in the above promise is the fact that the New Covenant is not confined to the Jews. Since it is written on the heart and mind instead of tablets of stone, it represents a spiritual relationship, not a fleshly one. It is, therefore, a relationship between God and spiritual Israel rather than the Jewish nation. It is intended for believers of all races and nations. Jews in the flesh come under the New Covenant through a changed mind and heart, as anyone else.

Second, the New Covenant is characterized by a personal and universal knowledge about God. Under this covenant, the privilege and obligation to learn of God is for everyone, not just for spiritual leaders. Neither is it merely a matter of racial descent or national character, but of individual concern. Under the New Covenant, the knowledge of God involves personal instruction and learning, spiritual rebirth, and individual commitment.

Third, the mark of the New Covenant is the provision for forgiveness of sins. The daily sacrifices of the Old Testament system as well as the sacrifice of the Day of Atonement provided no adequate remission of sins, but actually reminded the people of their sins. Under the New Covenant, on the other hand, there is total forgiveness through the blood of Christ.

Through our relationship to Him, based on God's grace and man's faith instead of human effort, God completely removes our sins and blots them out of His memory.

Having quoted from Jeremiah to illustrate the greater promises of the New Covenant, the Hebrews writer finally and simply concluded that the prophet's mere mention of the New Covenant antiquated the Old and implied that it was to be superseded. Some New Testament scholars believe that the writer's further assertion that the covenant with the Jews "is obsolete and aging [and] will soon disappear" is also a reference to the priestly and sacrificial systems, and is ample proof that he wrote before A.D. 70. Others do not consider this statement to mean necessarily that the temple was still standing or that sacrifices were still being offered. He could merely have meant that from the time the New was predicted, the end of the Old Covenant was unmistakably signified in Jeremiah's prophecy of the New Covenant.

Lessons From Chapter Seven

Good, Better, Best

A Better Tabernacle

The place of Jewish worship was called at first a tabernacle and at last a temple. Whichever you call it, it was a good one. There is, however, a better temple. The first was on earth. The second is in Heaven. The first had a human priest. The second has the Lord of glory as its Priest. The first demanded annual sacrifices. The second accepts the sacrifice of Jesus made once and for all. The first had literal sacrifices; the second, spiritual sacrifices. The first required the death of animals. The second is based on the death of the Divine Son of God. The first was preparatory. The second was permanent.

There is really no holy place on earth. Not in the sense of these verses. We may show respect for places where we meet God. We may treat with care places where God is praised in song or petitioned in prayer. But in the sense of our Scripture, these are not holy places. Even Israel is not truly our Holy Land. Our Holy Place is in Heaven. That is the center of our worship. That is where Christ, our High Priest, entered with His own blood. That is where the true and lasting mercy seat is. Not only is it a better tabernacle—it is the best tabernacle!

A Better Testament

The Old Testament was a good testament. The New Testament is a better testament. The old served its purpose, but its purposes have been achieved. The New Testament is a better testament because it has a better mediator. The mediator of the Old Testament was a man; the mediator of the New is the Master.

In 1983, the U.S.A. issued a postage stamp commemorating the building of the first steel bridge in America. It was extremely important to St. Louis to have this link across the Mississippi. The bridge was built by James Eads, even though many said such a bridge could not be built. They said it would never support the weight of its own steel. When it was finished, they still didn't trust it. So Eads drove fourteen locomotives across it all at the same time! They called it the eighth wonder of the world! Jesus is the bridge we cross to get to God. It filled a great need. No one else was able to provide adequate access to God. Many said it wouldn't work. It is the supreme wonder of the world. The word "mediator" comes to us from law and religion, and it explains Christ's role adequately. The word "bridge" comes from everyday life and shows Christ's work unmistakably unmistakable!

Oscar Wilde wrote in *De Profundis:*

There is still something to me almost incredible in the idea of a young Galilean peasant imagining that he could bear on his own shoulders the burden of the entire world: all that had already been done and suffered; the sins of Nero, of Caesar Borgia, of Alexander VI, and of him who was emperor of Rome and priest of the sun; the sufferings of those whose names are legion and whose dwelling is among the tombs; oppressed nationalities, factory children, thieves, people in prison, outcasts, those who are dumb under oppression and whose silence is heard only of God; and not merely imagining this but actually achieving it, so that at the present moment all who come in contact with his personality... find that the ugliness of their sin is taken away and the beauty of their sorrow revealed to them.

The New Testament is a better testament because it has better promises. The first promises were national; the second are personal. The first was regional; the second, universal. The first, temporary; the second, eternal. When you read the Old Testament, it speaks of climatic conditions that do not apply to all the world, of social conditions that do not apply to all the world, of social conditions that do not apply to all time, of political conditions that apply only to that certain portion of history.

When you read the New Testament, you see at once that it applies to people of every land and language and of every age. Not only is it a better testament, it is the best testament!

A Better Tablet

Man has always been looking for a better tablet. He wrote on papyrus, but it would not last. He wrote on parchment, the skins of animals. That was some improvement. He wrote on stones. That lasts a long time, but it finally fades. Have you ever tried to read the dates on an old tombstone? When they sent Pioneer II into space, they put on it a plaque so that should it be found by inhabitants of some other world, they would know it came from earth. They engraved their symbolic message on plates of gold! The better testament is written on the tablets of the heart. That is more lasting, more personal, more effective, more practical, and more touching! Not only is it a better tablet, it is the best tablet.

CHAPTER EIGHT

Superior Sanctuary and Ritual

Hebrews 9:1-28

The Earthly Tabernacle and Its Ritual (9:1-10)

The Hebrews writer continued in chapter 9 to emphasize the greater ministry of Christ under the new order. In the preceding chapter, the superior place of His ministry and the better promises of the covenant under which He serves were discussed. Here the reader is exposed to a more thorough contrast between the sanctuary and priestly ritual under the two covenants. Continuing to affirm the superiority of the real to the unreal, the author kept before his readers the background idea that the old sanctuary, ritual, and priesthood were only transitory figures of their true counterparts under the new. Their very physical and material nature testified to their temporary character.

The earthly tabernacle proper was divided into two rooms. The first of these was the Holy Place, in which the priests ministered. Two articles of furniture occupied this area. The seven-branched candlestick, located on the south side of the room, was made of one piece of pure gold. It was dressed daily. On the north side was the table of shewbread, made of acacia wood and overlaid with gold. On it were placed twelve loaves (the "bread of presence") that were renewed each Sabbath.

Separating the Holy Place from the Holy of Holies, named the Most Holy Place in this chapter, was a curtain made of blue, purple, and scarlet. Some question has arisen among students of Hebrews concerning why the writer placed the golden censor inside the Holy of Holies, whereas in Exodus 30:6 the altar of incense is located in the Holy Place just before the veil separating the two. One possible explanation is that he was referring to the incense from off the altar, without which the high priest did not enter the Holy of Holies on the Day of Atonement. It may be a reference to the smoke pan containing the coals from the altar of incense that he used on that day. The pan was kept in a side chamber at the entrance to the Holy of Holies.

Of course, the most important article in the inner sanctuary was the ark of the covenant. It was a box made of acacia wood and overlaid inside and out with gold. It contained the pot of manna (see Exodus 16:33), Aaron's rod that budded (Numbers 17:1-10), and the two tablets of stone on which

God had inscribed the Ten Commandments at Horeb (Exodus 34:1-4). On the ark lay a slab of gold called the mercy seat, on which the blood of the atoning sacrifice and the sin offering were sprinkled on the Day of Atonement. In one piece with the mercy seat, and rising above it, were two golden cherubim with outspread wings and faces turned toward each other. Between them glowed the perpetual Shekinah glory, which symbolized the very presence of God. (See Exodus 25:18-22.)

Many worthwhile things could be written about the typology of the tabernacle and its furnishings. The author of the letter at this point was more concerned about the failure of the priestly services performed in and with them to provide any lasting satisfaction for the people. In the Holy Place, only the priests officiated and ministered before God. The Holy of Holies was open to the high priest alone, who entered it only once a year, on the tenth day of the seventh month. Even then he did not enter without sin offerings of the blood of the slain bull for himself and his household on the first entrance, and the blood of the slaughtered goat for the sins of the people on the second. (See Leviticus 16.)

In this manner, the tabernacle and its sacrificial arrangements actually constituted a barrier to the people's access to God. While furnishing a constant reminder of their sin, it offered no means for them to enter God's presence. Dealing with physical and ceremonial cleansings of the flesh, it offered no purifying of the conscience from dead works. After all, it was intended to provide the people only a limited access to God and temporary satisfaction of conscience until Christ would come.

The Superior Sacrifice of the New Covenant (9:11-14)

The contrast between the shadow-like earthly Jewish tabernacle and the greater, divinely constructed, and absolutely perfect one in which Christ serves as high priest is further magnified by the superior sacrifice by which He has made His entrance into the Heavenly sanctuary. The sacrifice that Jesus has made was not the sin offering of bulls and goats that Aaron and the Jewish high priests offered for themselves and the people, and by the blood of which they entered yearly on the Day of Atonement into the Holy of Holies. Nor was it the ashes of the slaughtered and burned perfect red heifer by which ceremonial impurity was removed from one who had had contact with a dead body (Numbers 19). Rather, Jesus sacrificed His own blood. Through it, He opened the way to the Heavenly tabernacle and entered it once to stay.

The writer of Hebrews may have been suggesting that, completing the sacrifice of His own blood on the cross, Christ, in a spiritual sense, carried

His blood with Him into Heaven. There He now offers it up for the sins of His people. By this explanation, the blood of Christ plays a continuing vital role in His intercessory ministry.

In any case, there is a great difference between the sacrifice of animals under the old system and the eternally redemptive sacrifice of Christ under the new. The blood of animals effected only an outward ceremonial sanctification of the flesh. It allowed the Jews to participate in worship, but they could only draw as near to God as the limitations of their priestly ritual would allow. The blood of Christ cleanses the conscience of the believer, allowing him to draw near in worshipful service to God. His life becomes one unbroken worship experience through Christ.

Christ the Mediator of a More Excellent Covenant (9:15-28)

Through the sacrifice of His blood, Christ became the mediator of a new and better covenant. (See Matthew 26:28 and 1 Corinthians 11:25.) Yet even as His death provided the great promise of a glorious inheritance for those under the New, Covenant, it was also effective for the sins of those under the Old. To the ones who obeyed God's commandments, who looked beyond Joshua to Jesus, beyond Moses to Christ, beyond law to grace, and who perceived the spiritual realm by faith, the sacrifice of Jesus Christ was retroactively efficacious in redeeming their transgressions. (See 1 Corinthians 10:4; Hebrews 11:10, 13-16, 26; 12:23.)

This eternal inheritance that was promised under the New Covenant rested on the death of Christ, as the fulfillment of any legacy is contingent on the death of the testator. The word that has been translated "covenant" up to this point may also be defined "will" or "testament" in a juristic sense, and must surely mean that in verses 15 and 16, or else the meaning of the writer is difficult to understand. Just as the conditions of a will become legally binding only after the death of the one who made the testament, so the death of our Lord was necessary for the promised inheritance to pass on to believers.

The Hebrews writer recounted in some detail that even the Mosaic Covenant was ratified with blood, although it was not the blood of the one who made it. This sealing of the covenant between the people and God, by the blood of animals, was a type of the reconciliation of man to God that was accomplished through the death of Jesus. (See 2 Corinthians 5:18-21.)

The Biblical account of the inauguration of the Old Covenant records that Moses took the blood of oxen and sprinkled it on the altar and on the people (Exodus 24:3-8). It is interesting to note that the writer of Hebrews also mentioned the blood of goats, the sprinkling of blood on the scroll, and the use of water, scarlet wool, and hyssop. The fact that the latter items are not found in the Exodus story, however, is no indication that they were not a part of that event. The blood of goats, which was associated with the sin offering for the people on the Day of Atonement (Leviticus 16:9, 15), could also have been used at the institution of the covenant, and the sprinkling of the scroll would not be out of keeping with the other things consecrated with blood. Hyssop was sometimes used as a sprinkling brush. Water, scarlet, and hyssop are joined with blood for ceremonial cleansings on other occasions. (See Exodus 12:22; Leviticus 14:4-7, 49-52; Numbers 19.)

There were surely innumerable historical incidents related to the history of God's people that were not recorded in the Old Testament. It may very well be that the Hebrews writer was referring to details that were commonly known among the Jews in his day but were not a part of the Exodus account. It may be that under divine inspiration, he related parts of the actual narrative that Moses had not reported.

Some students of this book also wonder at the author's reference to the sprinkling of the tabernacle and its vessels, since it was not yet constructed at the time the Old Covenant was instituted. This question arises, however, in part because of the unwarranted assumption that the Hebrews writer was describing just one historical incident in verses 18-21. Actually he may have been referring to both the ratification, or sealing, of the covenant in Exodus 24:3-8 and the dedication of the tabernacle in Exodus 40:9.

Such an answer is not altogether free of difficulty. The Exodus40 account of the tabernacle dedication, indicates that the tabernacle and its furnishings were sprinkled with oil on that occasion. There is no blood mentioned. The probable solution to the problem lies in the fact that oil and blood were used together for ceremonial consecration. For instance, Aaron and his sons were to be smeared with blood and anointed with oil when they were consecrated for priestly service (Exodus 29; Leviticus 8). Josephus, in his *Antiquities,* records that the tabernacle and its vessels were purified with blood and oil when they were dedicated.

The writer's conclusion was that "nearly everything" that was to be cleansed under the law had to be purified with blood, and without it there was to be no redemption from sin. These words fit so well those of our Lord in Matthew 26:28, "This is my blood of the covenant, which is poured out for many for the forgiveness of sins." Examples of the reason for the use of "nearly everything" are to be found in such places as Numbers 31:22-24, in which fire and water were used for purifying captured metal objects, and Leviticus 5:11-13, where a tenth of an ephah of fine flour is allowed as a sin offering for the poor.

Whereas "nearly everything" under the law, including the shadowy earthly tabernacle and its furnishings, had to be cleansed with the blood of animals, it was necessary that the Heavenly prototypes be consecrated with better sacrifices. Thus Christ, the better sacrifice, has entered into the Heavenly sanctuary, there to appear before God on our behalf.

Jesus' intercessory ministry, therefore, is further contrasted with that of the Levitical high priests. While they went into the Holy of Holies annually with the blood of others, Jesus' entrance into the Heavenly sanctuary followed the offering of himself once, finally and completely, to remove sin. His death is never to be repeated. Just as men are destined to die once and then later appear before God in judgment, so Christ has died once. When He reappears, it will not be to offer himself for sin again, a work already completed, but to receive to eternal salvation those who have accepted His redemption and eagerly anticipate His return.

Lessons From Chapter Eight

"A Superior Rating"

A Superior Sanctuary

The Jewish temple was truly a magnificent example of art and architecture for its time and place. However, it would hardly compare with some of the other temples that have been built. The Christian cathedrals that have been built across Europe dazzle the eye. The world's best architectural skills and artistry have combined to create some magnificent examples of man's devotion to his God. But nothing on earth can ever compare with the sanctuary in Heaven. That's the true Christian sanctuary. It will make St. Peter's Cathedral in Rome and St. Paul's Cathedral in London look very simple and ordinary. The magnificent old church of St. Sophia in Istanbul and the marvelous new cathedral in Coventry, England, will both be pauperized by the splendor of the Heavenly sanctuary into which Jesus has already entered and which we ourselves hope to enter someday.

The word *sanctuary* is also used in another sense. It is used to mean, not a place of worship, but a place of refuge. Of course, there was a time in history when the place of worship doubled as a place of refuge. A house of worship was regarded as holy ground. If a person could reach a church building, he could find refuge behind its doors. It was literally a sanctuary in the sense of a place of safety. It was here that David fled when being pursued by Absalom. Hundreds in Europe found refuge behind the doors of a house of worship. In this sense, too, the new provides a better sanctuary.

If, as Psalm 46 says, God is our refuge, then the better we know God, the more secure we are in refuge. The fuller revelation of the New Testament gives us a blessed assurance that is deeper and richer and finer than anything that could have been enjoyed under the old system.

A Superior Sacrifice

Under the Old Testament, every worshiper had to bring his own lamb. If he had no lamb, he had to buy a lamb. He could not borrow a lamb. Someone could not give him a lamb to use for the sacrifice. He could not steal a lamb for the sacrifice. It had to cost him something. He had to provide his own lamb. Suddenly, in the New Testament, everything is reversed. God provides the Lamb! It is not provided by the worshiper but by the One who is worshiped! It is not provided by the offender but by the One offended! It is not provided by the sinner but by the Savior!

Communion recreates this for us, for Communion is an act of God. We prepare the bread and wine. We set the table. We dress and come and sing and pray; but Communion is not our act. It is an act of God. God acted in giving His Son. God acted in instituting the service. God acts in meeting His children there.

So the sacrifice made for our sins is superior because of the One who made it. It is superior because of the moral character and nature of the One who made it. We have all read in the newspapers about some fire or flood that has threatened animals. We have read that some man risked his life to save an animal; and we have said that it would have been a shame if a human life were lost to rescue a brute beast. But Christ stands much farther above us than we stand above animals. How vast then must be the distance between animal sacrifices and Christ's sacrifices!

A Superior Salvation

Somewhere in America there is a town called New Canaan. But the Biblical promised land for Christians is not on this earth. The New Jerusalem comes down from Heaven! It will be more lasting than that territory promised to the children of Israel of old. It will be more peaceful than the earthly Jerusalem can possibly be. Isn't it ironic that the city whose very name means "peace" has known less of it than any city in history! Our promised land is Heaven. That is the new Eden toward which we move.

Some years ago, the cities of Spray, Leaksville, and Draper, North Carolina, merged. They called the new city Eden, North Carolina, because early explorers had described the area as a paradise. Of course, there is no earthly paradise. Our inheritance is in Heaven, but Heaven is New Canaan, New Jerusalem, and New Eden all in one!

So our better territory is really the best territory. But we do not have to wait for it. "All things are yours" says the Bible (1 Corinthians 3:21).

In one of J. Wilbur Chapman's evangelistic meetings, a man described his earlier life. He was a tramp. He got off the train in New York City and begged on the streets for a year. One day, he tapped a man on the shoulder and said, "Buddy, could you spare a dime?" The man turned around. It was his own father. "A dime! I have been looking for you for eighteen years. All that I have is yours!"

CHAPTER NINE

All-sufficient Sacrifice

Hebrews 10:1-18

Levitical Sacrifices and the Sacrifice of Christ (10:1-10)

The writer introduced in chapters 7 and 9 the contrast between the repeated and inadequate sacrifices of the Levitical system and the once-for-all and perfect nature of Christ's offering of himself. In chapter 9, he summarized that contrast and underscored the distinctive features of our Lord's sacrifice. His intention was to show conclusively that God's own purpose was that His Son alone would be the acceptable and complete sacrifice for sin.

The shadowy Levitical system of the Jews was a type of "good things that [were] coming," the death of Christ and His high-priestly ministry. The very fact that the animal sacrifices had to be offered repeatedly was testimony enough that they did not give perfect redemption to the worshipers or remove the consciousness of sin and guilt. True cleansing of sin, which involves the purifying of the conscience, is once for all. The annual sin offerings of the Day of Atonement were actually a yearly reminder of sins, not a remover of them. An atonement that has to be repeated is not a complete atonement. As the Hebrews writer concluded, this failure of the Levitical system merely substantiates the obvious truth that the blood of animals cannot remove moral guilt and provide assurance of forgiveness. The one sacrifice, on the other hand, that could completely atone for sins and take them away forever was made by Christ himself. (See Romans 5:11.)

Of course, none of the above discussion, or the Hebrew letter itself, was designed to minimize or obscure the value of the Levitical sacrifices as types of Christ. Through Him, forgiveness would come even to those in the Old Testament who offered their sacrifices in true faith to God. (1) They did keep alive an awareness of sin. This contribution was vital to the preparation for the coming of Christ. (2) They testified to the coming of something better.

Their very inadequacies were living prophecies of the advent of the perfect. (3) They did grant a temporary satisfaction to the worshiper and provide a limited access to God through the priestly ministry.

To substantiate his claim that Christ alone was the acceptable sacrifice, the Hebrews writer appealed to Psalm 40:6-8. In this Old Testament passage, Christ, addressing His Father, said that God was not pleased with burnt offerings and sin offerings, but delights in those who do His will. Most students of Hebrews are anxious to explain that the writer, in referring to the words of the psalmist, was not condemning sacrifice of dumb animals. Yet, too often these sacrifices were made without sincere faith and commitment on the part of the worshiper. The sacrifice of obedience, the sacrifice of a rational and spiritual being, was performed when Christ came into this world, in the body that His Father had prepared for Him, and offered himself. In so carrying out the will of God, He nullified the old order, inaugurated the new, and provided the sanctification from sin that the old had failed to effect.

An application can be made at this point concerning the relationship between salvation and the daily service of Christians. One is not acceptable to God because he makes sacrifices of time, talent, money, or anything else to God. The sacrifice for sin and salvation has already been made by Christ. His offering was complete and sufficient. Only by accepting His Son can one be received of the Father. The only sacrifice that He expects in return is that of a life submitted in worship to Him (Romans 12:1, 2). Time, talent, and money used in service to Him will naturally follow, not as sacrifices to God, but as expressions of the faith of one who has received life through the redemptive work of Christ and has yielded himself to Him.

The Exalted Christ (10:11-18)

In Hebrews 10:11, the writer was referring to the daily offerings of the priests in contrast to the sacrifices of the Day of Atonement in verses 1-4. A final contrast between the incomplete service of the Levitical priesthood and the perfect ministry of Christ was drawn from the positions that they assumed while performing their duties in representing the people before God. The law of Moses required that the Jewish priests always stand in the tabernacle and from that position minister and offer their sacrifices daily. Christ, however, after He had made His once-for-all sacrifice, sat down on the right hand of His Father in Heaven. Surely referring to Psalm 110:1, the Hebrews writer also noted that Jesus will maintain that position until His enemies are destroyed. (See also 1 Corinthians 15:22-28.)

One should be careful to understand that, in describing this superior characteristic of the sacrifice and ministry of Christ, the Hebrews writer was not contradicting the present intercessory ministry of Christ, which had already been discussed in chapters 4, 7, and 9. The reference to our Lord's sitting on the right hand of His Father was not meant to imply that He is resting from His work of mediation, but that He has a position of superior honor from which to perform that ministry.

Perhaps it would be well to list in summary fashion the contrasts between the sacrificial systems of the two covenants. (1) The Old was a shadow; the New is real. (2) The Levitical priests and high priests used animals; Christ offered himself. (3) The old system, while providing a limited access to God, constituted a barrier between Him and the people; the sacrifice of Christ under the new has opened the way for the people to approach God. (4) The blood of the Old Testament sacrifices, though providing a temporary satisfaction for sin, only effected ceremonial purification; the blood of Christ cleanses the conscience and removes the guilt of sin. (5) Under the Old Covenant, sacrifices were slaughtered repeatedly; Christ died once. (6) The sacrifices of the Old were a reminder of sins; the sacrifice of the New removes the sin forever. (7) The Levitical priests stood as they made their offerings; Christ sat down at the right hand of the Father after He had given himself.

By the perfect sacrifice of himself, Christ has accomplished what the old order could not. He has by His one offering provided absolute redemption and made "perfect" those who are sanctified by His blood. This is not to say, of course, that believers are perfect in the sense that they can do no wrong. It is to say that they have experienced full salvation, and, as long as they continue in Him, that salvation remains complete.

Jeremiah predicted this great truth in his prophecy (31:31-34). Attributing the prophet's words to the Holy Spirit, the Hebrews writer showed conclusively that even in the Old Testament, God had promised that under the New Covenant, sins would be removed forever. That promise has been fulfilled in Jesus. Through Him, God treats the believer's sins as if they had never been committed. If full forgiveness of sin has, therefore, been achieved, there is no need for further sacrifice. God has brought an end to it himself through the death of His Son.

Lessons From Chapter Nine

Something Old, Something New

It is a part of American wedding customs that the bride should wear "something old and something new." We borrow the phrase here to use in a very different way. In chapter 10's text, something old and something new are laid side by side that we may learn from the comparison. Often the old must give way to the new. That's the case with transportation, communication, housing, cooking, education, and medicine. The microwave oven has revolutionized cooking. No physician uses leeches any more. The old has given way to the new.

But the old does not give way to the new just because it is new. Some are turning back to old ways and finding them better. Wood stoves are coming back to heat American homes. The sun heats water as it must have done for the cave man. People are walking again and finding it a very excellent means of transportation. The old must give way to the new only if the old has outlived its usefulness and the new is manifestly better.

Even so, the Old Covenant was not replaced by the New simply because of the latter's novelty, but because of its superiority. In fact, there would have been no New Covenant if it were not a better covenant (Hebrews 8:7). But the New is better than the Old because it has substance, because it depends on submission to the all-sufficient sacrifice of Christ, because it covers sin and sanctifies the believer. To that, the Old must give way.

Shadow and Substance

We can determine the time by a shadow. Shortening shadows tell us noon is approaching; lengthening shadows tell us night is near. That was refined with the sun dial by means of which the shadow marks the hour. Shadows give us our bearings, pointing east or west like a compass. We learn much about earth by studying its shadow cast on the moon. The Old Testament and its worship are the shadow. As a man approaching from the sun casts his shadow before Him, so the substance of the New Testament was foreshadowed in the Old. When we interpret Scripture, the shadow gives us our bearings, for we must know whether the events occurred under the shadow of the Old or in the sunlight ("Son-light") of the New. The shadow of the Old served to prepare for the substance of the New. It was only when it was obvious that the Old wouldn't work that the New could be appreciated. (Hebrews 10:1). Like the natural shadows, the shadows of the Old Testament educate us. All of the terminology, symbols, and concepts of the New Testament would have little meaning if we had not been educated by the Old.

But the substance is Christianity, not Judaism. Shadows pass away; substances remain. Shadows are temporary, substances are permanent. It is a distinction that is fundamental to our understanding of Scripture, of history, and of ourselves.

Sacrifice and Submission (10:1-7)

We cannot say that sacrifice was limited to the old way and submission to the new. We *can* say that sacrifice was the center of the old and submission is the center of the new. There was submission in the old. "The sacrifices of God are a broken spirit; a broken and contrite heart, O God, you will not despise" (Psalm 51:17). "To obey is better than sacrifice, and to heed is better than the fat of rams" (1 Samuel 15:22). Those are *Old* Testament passages. In spite of that, in the common mind, the heart of Jewish worship was the sacrifice of animals. If that were not so, then those verses would not have been needed. We wonder how many thousands upon thousands of lambs were offered on the altars of Israel. How startling it must have been to those Hebrews to learn that "it is *impossible* for the blood of bulls and goats to take away sin" (Hebrews 10:4).

If submission is not limited to the New, sacrifice is not limited to the Old. The whole thrust of this chapter is that Christ made the only truly effective sacrifice for sin. But the things that made Christ's sacrifice effective were His sinlessness and His submission. No lamb went willingly to the altars of Israel. Christ went willingly to the cross. No lamb went knowingly to the altars of Israel. Christ went knowingly to the cross. If the lamb was the *emblem* of innocence, Jesus was the embodiment of innocence! It is the knowing, willing, innocent sacrifice that takes away sin!

For us, sacrifice *is* submission! Romans 12:1, 2: "Therefore, I urge you, brothers, in view of God's mercy, to offer your bodies as living sacrifices, holy and pleasing to God—this is your spiritual act of worship. Do not conform any longer to the pattern of this world, but be transformed by the renewing of your mind." The only sacrifice we make is our submission. And we do not make it to pay for our sins. We make it because He has already paid for our sins.

Sin-Covering and Sanctification

"Blessed is he whose transgressions are forgiven, whose sins are covered" (Psalm 32:1). We have often said the sins before Christ were only rolled back or held in abeyance, since only Christ's blood is effective. We have sometimes said they were "rolled forward." That is quite true, but that is seeing the thing from God's viewpoint. From man's standpoint, forgiveness in Old Testament times was just as real and full and complete as it is now. David was really forgiven. Abraham was fully forgiven. Isaiah says, "Though your sins are like scarlet, they shall be as white as snow; though they are red as crimson, they shall be like wool (1:18). Forgiveness under the Old Testament was real. Nor was sanctification missing in the old plan. If you read carefully the first five books of the Bible, you will find that buildings were sanctified, garments were sanctified, deeds were sanctified, and people were sanctified. One can easily deduce from that, that sanctification means to be set apart for a holy purpose.

How does the New improve on the Old? With regard to sin-covering, it looks back on a deed already done rather than forward on a deed yet to be done. There is no difference in the quality of the forgiveness, but there is an enormous difference in the quality of the assurance of forgiveness. How is sanctification better in the New? Sanctification in the New has nothing to do with ritual or ceremony. It deals instead with the sharp facts of everyday life. Those who are sanctified see all of life as a ministry, every hour of time as a stewardship, and every personal encounter as an opportunity to serve!

Quite recently, a very famous television evangelist advertised a special prime-time program. The title was, "What do you want God to do in your life?" That is very much the wrong question. Sanctification asks: "What does God want me to do with the life He has given me!

Part Four:

Faith in the Author of the Preeminent Way

CHAPTER TEN

Admonition to Faithfulness

Hebrews 10:19-39

Access to God Through Christ (10:19-25)

Hebrews 10:18 concludes the "theological" section of this treatise. The closing chapters follow with practical applications of its truths to the needs and problems of its first readers. Much of the previous part of the letter has dealt with the sacrifice and high priesthood of Christ under the New Covenant. Here the discussion turns to what those things should mean to readers in their present *circumstances.*

On the basis of the access to God that His Son has made available through His death and His present intercessory ministry for them, the Hebrew Christians were encouraged to draw near to God with boldness and confidence. They had already received the same admonition in 4:14-16. When His flesh was rent, Christ opened the curtain into God's presence, the inner sanctuary. Now believers can come to God through this "new and living way" with the full assurance that He will receive them through His Son's blood.

This glorious privilege is in striking contrast to the denial of entry into the Holy of Holies by those under the Old Covenant, with the exception of the high priest, who could go in only once a year. Moreover, the description of the way into God's presence, presented in verse 20, is strongly reminiscent of the Gospel account of the rending of the curtain separating the Holy Place and the Holy of Holies in the temple when Christ died on the cross (Matthew 27:51; Mark 15:38; Luke 23:45). It also reminds us of the words of Jesus that He is the "way and the truth and the life" and that no one can come to the Father except by Him (John 14:6).

The condition under which one can respond to the exhortation to draw near to God is that his heart is cleansed from an evil conscience and his body washed with pure water. While mere ceremonial purification of the flesh by the blood of animal sacrifices under the Old Covenant could not meet that condition, the cleansing of the conscience through the blood of Christ can and does. 'The writer may have had in mind the similarity between the ceremonial cleansing of the priest to purify him for ministry in the tabernacle (Exodus 29) and the cleansing in baptism that the believer experiences in his entry into the service of the priesthood of believers.

There can be little doubt that in verse 22, the author of Hebrews was referring to Christian baptism. As Peter suggests, baptism is more than merely the washing of the body; it is also the "pledge of a good conscience toward God" (1 Peter 3:21). In this divinely authorized expression of one's faith in Christ and His gift of grace, the believer is born again, "born of water and the Spirit" (John 3:5). Thus he experiences the "washing of rebirth, and renewal by the Holy Spirit" (Titus 3:5). His body is washed with water, and through the Holy Spirit, his heart is made new by the blood of Christ.

The Hebrew Christians were also encouraged to hold unswervingly to the hope they professed, placing their trust in, and receiving strength from, the faithfulness of God. The importance of this admonition to persevere in one's confidence in God and the confession of it is evident from the number of times that it is repeated in this letter. (See 3:6, 14; 4:14.) It is a truth that one cannot possibly emphasize too much.

Another exhortation in this text is that Christians concentrate on helping each other, not themselves, by stimulating one another to "love and good deeds." Christianity is an experience of fellowship. It needs a society, ordained and established by God, in which to express itself. Withdrawing from the Christian community and staying away from the gathering of believers will not meet this need for the Christian. Some students of the Hebrew letter suggest that some of the Christians were staying away because of what they considered their superior knowledge of God's revelation. Others suggest that they were afraid of persecution. Another Supposition is that they were simply becoming negligent and indifferent. The ones to whom the letter was addressed were warned not to follow their example of shunning the congregation.

The writer implied that the assembly of the church is designed, to a large extent, for sharing. It is not so much an event to which one goes to get something as it is a fellowship in which we gather to share. The church of today would do well to create an atmosphere in which the members participate more in the difficulties of each other and help one another more. Surely this is what the having of "everything in common" in Acts 2 and 4 was all about.

Most students of Hebrews suggest that the "Day approaching," toward which they were to look as they encouraged each other, was the destruction of Jerusalem in A.D. 70, the return of Christ, or the Day of Judgment ("day of the Lord" in Scripture). There are others, however, who believe it to be the Lord's Day, the day of the assembly, which some of them were forsaking and needed to be exhorted to keep.

The Sin of Apostasy (10:26-31)

The neglecting of the assembly of the church must have been the outward mark of a more serious condition on the part of some of these Hebrew Christians. On the other hand, the writer may have been suggesting that absenting oneself from the gatherings of the believers may lead to a more serious state of sin. Perhaps he meant to convey both of the above ideas. At any rate, he warned them against the dreadful sin of apostasy, the willful sin of renouncing the Christian faith after one has "received the knowledge of the truth." Surely he had in mind the same condition that he described in 6:4-8. As he did in that earlier text, the author was speaking here, not of a case of merely yielding to a temptation or postbaptismal sin, but of outright and deliberate rejection of the salvation that one has experienced in Christ. To do this is to trample underfoot the Son of God, to count His atoning blood by which one is sanctified as the most common thing, and to treat with scorn the Holy Spirit.

Such apostasy can result only in the severest judgment and condemnation on the part of God. Even a man who set at naught the law of Moses by the sin of idolatry, blasphemy, and any other grievous sin was to be stoned to death without mercy on the evidence of two or more people. (See Deuteronomy 17:2-7.) Apostasy from the Christian faith is still worse. To illustrate the awful gravity of the condemnation that would befall those who committed this apostasy, the writer quoted from Deuteronomy 32:35, 36 and 2 Samuel 24:14. While all of these Old Testament passages in verses 30 and 31 can imply the judgment with which God vindicates His people against their enemies, they also refer to the impartial and stern retribution that He executes against His children who forsake His covenant. This sobering truth calls to mind the solemn words of Peter: "For it is time for judgment to begin with the family of God; and if it begins with us, what will the outcome be for those who do not obey the gospel of God?" (1 Peter 4:17).

There Is Reason for Encouragement and Hope (10:32-39)

The author had been denouncing apostasy as the sin for which "no sacrifice for sin is left." Then he exhorted his readers to confidence and hope in the Christian faith by a reminder of their past history of persecutions and faithfulness. Difficulties were not new to them. Not long after they became Christians, some of them had suffered the affliction of public ridicule and derision because of their lives of faith. They had also patiently endured the plundering and spoiling of their property. They were convinced that their abiding possessions in Heaven were higher than temporary ones on earth. Others of their number had taken the part of those who had suffered such mistreatment and ministered unto them, visiting and helping them even when they were imprisoned. In all of this, however, none had suffered martyrdom (12:4).

The Hebrews had begun the Christian race of life very well by doing the will of God. Such a beginning should have encouraged them to patient endurance until they had received the reward. The Hebrews writer's quotations from Isaiah 26:20 and Habakkuk 2:3, 4 suggest that such endurance is only for a little while in the light of the certain return of the Lord, who will end all afflictions and bring His promised blessing. The blessing, however, will not be received by those who fall back, but by those who maintain their faith in Him. The writer was confident that his readers were numbered among the faithful rather than among those who fell back.

This brief reference to faith in the prophecy of Habakkuk introduces the great discussion of faith that follows in the next chapter. At a point in their history when the people were suffering under oppression and corruption on every hand, Habakkuk had cried out to God for an answer. The Lord responded, "The righteous will live by his faith." The Christian life does not find its support in what transpires around it. Faith is not a result of circumstances. Through faith one rises above circumstances and draws his strength from above. Thus, faith was the quality most needed by the Hebrew Christians in order to persevere in the temptations that faced them.

Lessons From Chapter Ten

Putting Feet on Your Faith

Here are verses to help us get faith down out of the clouds and onto the streets where we live. The verses, Hebrews 10:22-24, offer us three succinct directions: "Let us draw near," "Let us hold unswervingly," and "Let us consider … one another." The first has to do with the assurance of faith, the second with the profession of faith, the third with the expression of faith.

The Assurance of Faith

"Let us draw near." How startling that sounded to Hebrew Christians. Their whole Jewish tradition had said just the opposite: "Stand back." The architecture of their temple said it. There was an outer court for the Gentiles, an inner court for the women, an inmost court for the men. After that came the temple proper, which only priests could enter because it was a holy place. And within that, a Most Holy Place, which only the high priest could enter, but only once a year. The whole message of that architecture was, "Stand back!"

There were ranks of people to match their temple. The high priest stood next to God himself. The lesser priests represented the people before God. Then came the men. Then the women. Then the Gentiles. The whole arrangement said, "Stand back!"

Their rituals reflected it. The burnt offerings were offered at an open-air altar in the sight of all. But the altar of incense was inside the temple, seen only by the priests, and seen only dimly by them in that shadowy room lit by seven candles. When it came time to offer blood for the sins of the people, the high priest went alone into that Most Holy Place, which was shrouded in complete and perpetual darkness. Their rituals took them onto holier and holier ground and into deeper and deeper darkness. It was all calculated to say, "Stand back!"

Their history reflected it. When Moses received the law, they forbade anyone to climb Mount Sinai. They put a fence at the base lest anyone blunder upon it. It said, "Stand back!"

Now it was to *Hebrew* Christians who had always been told to stand back that the verse was written, "Let us draw near!" What a privilege! God is approachable! Now that humanity has learned the lesson of reverence, it is possible to teach the lesson of intimacy. God may never be approached casually, but He may be approached closely!

The Profession of Faith

"Let us hold unswervingly." The King James Version says we "hold fast the profession of our faith"; the New American Standard Bible says "to the confession of our hope." There is little difference between a profession and a confession. There is considerable difference, however, between faith and hope—but they are twin sisters. You cannot have hope without faith; and if you have faith, you must certainly have hope. They are so intertwined we may be sure that one will not object if the other gets the publicity!

We are to hold unswervingly or without wavering. There is to be no doctrinal wavering. New and strange doctrines keep coming along, but we must keep to the faith once delivered.

There must be no moral wavering. There is no sin that does not have its defenders. Some of them are organized, and some of them are militant; but all of them are wrong. Moral principles have not changed since Eden. They are the same now as then. You can trace them from Eden to Mt. Sinai and the Ten Commandments to Jesus in the Sermon on the Mount and to Paul in his epistles. We are not to waver in morality.

Nor are we to waver in our confidence. We are to stand on the promises. "Standing on the Promises" is more than the title to a popular gospel song with a catchy tune. It is the very heart of our religion. It is the only place we have to stand.

Once a song leader stopped a congregation in the middle of that song, "Standing on the Promises." He asked people in the audience to volunteer some of the promises on which they were standing. One said, "Lo, I am with you, always." Another said, "The blood of Jesus Christ his Son cleanseth us from all sin." Still another said, "Where two or three are gathered together, there am I in the midst." Soon, a dozen promises had been quoted. When the singing resumed, there was a marked increase in enthusiasm; and, surely, it must have been accompanied by a marked increase in understanding, too.

The Expression of Faith

"Let us consider ... one another." That third direction may not seem to fit in with the other two, but it does. There is a passage in the Russian novel *The Brothers Karamazov* that explains it. A woman has come to talk with a holy man about her problems with faith. "What if I've been believing all my life, and when I come to die there is nothing but Burdocks growing over my grave? ... How can I prove it? How can I convince myself?" The holy man's answer is, "By the experience of active love ... in so far as you advance in active love, you will grow surer of the reality of God and of the immortality of your soul."

So it fits admirably to add that we must express our faith by considering one another. It is said that until the turn of the last century, the major cause of death among infants of less than a year old was *marasmus.* The name comes from a Greek word that means "wasting away." It was used to describe children who were well fed, well clothed, and well housed, but who received no love or attention. How many babes in Christ die from *marasmus?* They waste away because no one shows concern for them.

Hettie Green was a famous millionaire. She lived in seclusion and became a virtual recluse. She had only a few friends and an ugly mongrel dog that kept biting the few friends she did have. One of them said, "You've got to get rid of that dog." Hettie Green refused. She said, "That dog loves me, and he doesn't even know how rich I am!" To love the rich and the poor, to show concern and consideration, is truly to express our Christian faith.

There is a surprising way to show that concern. It is to go to church. Surely, we know that when we are absent from worship, we hurt God. When God has given us the privilege denied to so many, when He has said to us, "Draw near," surely it is painful to Him that some spurn the invitation. When we miss worship, we hurt ourselves. We deny ourselves the spiritual nourishment we need. The surprising thing is that when we miss worship, we hurt others. We deny them the spiritual encouragement and support that they need.

There once was a man who had a room in his house that he kept locked. The family was forbidden to enter. When at last he died, they couldn't wait to get the key and go in. They found currency, collections of coins (both gold and silver), and uncashed checks—checks that now never could be cashed! How much of life is like an uncashed check? How many of life's opportunities do we fail to see and fail to seize?

CHAPTER ELEVEN

Encouragement From Faithful Examples

Hebrews 11:1-40

The Nature of Faith (11:1-3)

The King James version calls faith "the 'assurance' [the giving substance to] things hoped for and the 'conviction' [proof from testing] of things not seen." A theme running throughout Hebrews is that the world of the five senses is transitory, but true reality finds its basis in the unseen world. Faith is the means by which a Christian can grasp the invisible realm of the spirit and lay hold on the future fulfillment of God's promises while he resides bodily in the physical world.

According to the Hebrews writer, faith has two dimensions. It runs from us to God and from God to us. Like the elders of old, by faith we look to God beyond the seen to the unseen, and by the same means, we are made acceptable to Him and receive His commendation.

It should be carefully pointed out that the author of this letter was not suggesting that faith makes the unseen and promised worlds real. They are real apart from any man's faith. Faith, however, gives substance to the unseen worlds and enables the believer to experience them. In other words, although faith is not proof from reason or the testimony of the five senses, it is a genuine criterion of knowledge, the comprehension of true (spiritual) reality. For the Christian, it is a sixth sense. It is not merely that which carries one through when knowledge has failed, although it does frequently defy so-called human understanding. Faith is actually superior to the five senses as a standard of perception. By the senses, we perceive only the physical world of reason; by faith, we understand and experience the eternal truth of God.

The history of God's people furnishes ample evidence of this truth concerning the nature of faith. Before the Hebrews writer cited any of their experiences, however, he referred to the divine act of God that preceded history: the creation of the world. Without faith, even the origin of this physical world remains a mystery. By it, on the other hand, we perceive that the visible world was brought into being by God's Word. That the things that are seen came from that which is invisible can be known only by faith.

The Witnesses of Faith (11:4-40)

Abel was the first mentioned in the long list of those heroes of the past who lived by such faith. (See Genesis 4:2-7.) Suggested reasons as to why Abel's sacrifice was acceptable and his brother's was not vary. Some suppose it was because Abel's was a blood offering and Cain's, only the produce of the ground. Others believe that Abel's sacrifice represented a tithe, while Cain's did not. Whatever explanation may be given for the acceptance of the one brother's sacrifice and the rejection of the other's, the author of this letter made it clear that the basic reason was that Abel offered in faith. By his faith, he was righteous. Through his faith, he testifies even centuries after his death.

Enoch, the second example of faith in action, did not experience death but was taken up by God (Genesis 5:21-24). Some have suggested that, living in the midst of a visibly perverse and evil generation, Enoch by faith walked above it with the invisible God and eventually was taken up by Him. In any case, it was his faith that made him well-pleasing to God. In fact, no one can please God without faith. To approach Him and be received by Him, anyone must believe that God exists and that He will bless those who seek Him.

Responding to a divine directive concerning things invisible, Noah reverently obeyed God and built the ark. In doing so, he saved his family and, by his faith, became an heir of righteousness and condemned the unbelieving and disobedient world around him. His experience gave ample testimony to the truth that the entrance of light always constitutes a judgment of the darkness that surrounds it.

No roll call of the faithful could possibly be taken without including Abraham. Because of his confidence in God, he left his home country and went into the strange and unknown land of Canaan, to which his Heavenly Father had called him and which he would receive as an inheritance. When Abraham arrived in the land, he patiently dwelt in tents and wandered uncomplainingly from place to place with his family, because he looked in faith to the invisible Heavenly and eternal city "whose architect and builder is God." Because of this same trust in God's promises, he and Sarah defied the law of nature and had a child when they were too old to do so. Thus, from a man who was the same as dead, as far as bringing children into the world was concerned, there issued descendants as numerous as the stars in the sky and the sand on the seashore.

There were two characteristics of Abraham's faith that were also manifested in the lives of the other great men of faith described in this chapter. First, his faith was often displayed in opposition to reason. In faith, Abraham responded to God's call and took the illogical step of going out, "even though he did not know where he was going." Contrary to scientific evidence, he trusted God to give him a child when he and his wife were past age. As the writer described later, Abraham expressed the same absurd (by human standards) confidence in God when he determined to offer his own son as a blood sacrifice. The second obvious mark of Abraham's faith was that it resulted in simple obedience. By faith he obeyed, went out, sojourned, looked for a city, and responded to still more demanding commands of God.

Most people's conduct can be accounted for on the basis of the circumstances that surround them. On the other hand, one of the mysteries of the Christian faith is that it frees one from conformity to this world (Romans 12:2) and often prompts him to act in a way contrary to the logic that worldly evidence would dictate. It is little wonder that Paul could say, "We are fools for Christ" (1 Corinthians 4:10). Faith like Abraham's will also cause one to take God at His word and act accordingly. If there is no response to God's commands, faith is void. Unbelief and disobedience are practically synonymous; they spring from the same stem. For God to command is for the man of faith to obey. Failure to do so is practical atheism.

These all (Abraham, Sarah, Isaac, and Jacob) died long before the promises that God made to them would be ultimately fulfilled in Christ, but they perceived them "from a distance" and "welcomed them." Further, having no fixed foothold on earth, and having received a divine call to a spiritual inheritance, they confessed that they were strangers and pilgrims in this world. They were looking for a permanent home, and Canaan was not their goal. Nor was the land of Ur, from which Abraham and his family had come, their true home. If so, they could easily have returned to it. No, their hearts were set on an unseen Heavenly city that God would build. Because they took God at His word and displayed such faith in Him, He "is not ashamed to be called their God." He was known, in fact, as "the God of Abraham, the God of Isaac and the God of Jacob" (Exodus 3:6). Their high reward is one that all children of God can receive.

Resuming his description of Abraham's faith, the writer of Hebrews called attention to the greatest example of the patriarch's trust and confidence in God's promises. He was willing to offer up his son Isaac, simply because God commanded him to. In spite of the unmistakable fact that God's promise to Abraham of countless posterity was to be fulfilled in Isaac, Abraham was ready to sacrifice the child of promise. He believed that if his son died, God would raise him from the dead in order to keep His promise. Genesis 22:5 makes it clear that Abraham expected to return from the mountain of sacrifice with Isaac. Through Abraham's faith, according to the writer of Hebrews, this experience was a kind of resurrection from the dead. Some see in this a foreshadowing of the resurrection of Jesus. (See John 8:56.)

By the same confidence in God and His promises, Isaac blessed his sons, Jacob and Esau, concerning the unseen things of the future. (See Genesis 27:1-40.) When Isaac learned that he had been deceived into giving Esau's blessing to Jacob, the aged patriarch manifested continuing faith in God's providence. He refused to withdraw the blessing from Jacob and bestowed a lesser blessing on Esau.

When he was old and near the point of death, leaning on his staff, Jacob likewise remained firm in his faith in God as he blessed his grandsons. For different reasons than his father's, Jacob also pronounced a greater blessing on the younger grandson, Ephraim, than on the older, Manasseh. In both cases, however, the patriarchs, through faith in God, blessed their sons "in regard to their future."

As his fathers before him had done, Joseph in turn demonstrated marvelous faith in the fulfillment of God's unseen promises to Abraham. Before he died and before the Israelites were ever brought under the oppression of the Pharaohs of Egypt, he made arrangements for his body to be taken to Canaan when the people of Israel returned. Under Moses, more than four hundred years later, Joseph's bones were removed from Egypt, as he had requested, and under Joshua they were placed in a burial spot in Shechem (Exodus 13:19; Joshua 24:32).

In his record of the Old Testament characters of faith, the author of Hebrews moved from the patriarchs to the great lawgiver, Moses. The faith of Moses, however, was preceded by that of his parents, Amram and Jochebed. They, perhaps realizing that God had destined their son to lead His people, defied the decree of Pharaoh that all newborn male Israelite children be put to death, and hid him for three months (Exodus 2:1, 2).

Pharaoh's daughter found Moses where his mother had hidden him and reared him as her son in the royal household. Moses later renounced the Egyptian court, with all of its position, advantage, comfort, and promise for the future. He identified himself with his despised and oppressed Israelite brothers (Exodus 2:3-15). Moses thus chose to share in the sufferings of his countrymen rather than enjoy the temporary pleasures of what had become to him a dishonorable position of privilege and prestige among their oppressors. He affirmed that "disgrace for the sake of Christ" was more valuable to him than the wealth of Egypt. "Disgrace for the sake of Christ" may refer to the identification of Christ with the experiences of His people even in Old Testament times. It may indicate that Moses suffered the disgrace that he did as he looked forward in faith to the coming of Christ. Or it may refer to the kind of disgrace that Christ would suffer when He came to earth. (See Psalm 69:9; 1 Corinthians 10:4.)

In any case, Moses looked in faith beyond the seen to the unseen, beyond the present to the future, to a greater reward than Egypt could offer. It is both ironic and in the providence of God that, in addition to the "reward" that he sought and received from his Maker, Moses also experienced greater earthly fame and glory than he could ever have achieved in the court of Pharaoh. There is in the life of Moses a great lesson in faith for any child of God who weighs present earthly pleasure against future reward in the face of God's commands and the requirements of His kingdom.

Although Moses fled to Midian when Pharaoh sought to slay him for killing the Egyptian who was smiting the Israelite, the Hebrews writer emphasizes that Moses did not leave Egypt because of fear of Pharaoh so much as faith in God. Perhaps he realized that the time was not right for God's deliverance of His people. The response of two of them to Moses' action would tend to support such an idea. (See Exodus 2:13, 14.) At any rate, Moses left Egypt because he looked in faith beyond the visible king of Egypt and held on with surety and certainty to the invisible King of Heaven and earth.

In this same spirit, Moses instituted the Passover. He led his people to sprinkle the blood of the paschal lamb on the lintels and doorposts of their houses on their last night in Egypt. The angel of doom would then pass by them as he brought death to the firstborn men and beasts of Egypt. Their faith in God's saving power through the sacrificial blood spared their firstborn from the destroyer. Likewise, our faith is in Christ, the Lamb of God of whom the Passover was a type (John 19:36; 1 Corinthians 5:7, 8). By that faith, we are freed from the destructive power of death.

Although the Exodus account of the Red Sea experience is marked by unbelief on the part of God's people, the author of Hebrews selects it as an example of faith. It may be that he is further emphasizing the faith of Moses, or perhaps he is showing that the people had to manifest some faith to move forward at Moses' command. The Egyptians perished for taking the same step because it was in opposition to the Word of God rather than a response of faith in Him. (See Exodus 14.)

It is interesting to note that in selecting incidents from the history of Israel to use as examples of faith, the inspired writer omitted any reference to the wilderness wanderings. This is perfectly natural, however, inasmuch as he had already referred many times in the letter to the wilderness experiences of unbelief.

The author did, however, mention the capture of Jericho, the first city to fall in the promised land, in his catalog of the great acts of faith. The wails of the city fell only after Joshua and the Israelites had explicitly followed the specific and detailed instructions of God. They were told to march around the city once each day for six days. Seven priests bearing seven trumpets and followed by the ark of the covenant would lead the procession each day. On the seventh day, the procedure was to be repeated seven times, concluding with a long trumpet blast and a great shout of all the people (Joshua 6:1-21).

In the destruction that followed, the only inhabitants who were spared were a harlot named Rahab and her family. She had believed in the power and providence of God. Trusting His people to save her, she had safely hidden two men whom Joshua had sent to spy on Jericho and had secured their escape from the city when their presence there became known (Joshua 2; 6:22-25). She is mentioned elsewhere in Scripture as an ancestress of Jesus (Matthew 1:5) and as an example of righteousness (James 2:25).

Following the mention of Rahab, the Hebrews writer concluded his description of the men and events of faith from the history of Israel with a summary enumeration of men and deeds in the periods of the judges, kings, and prophets.

It is interesting to note that of the six men mentioned by name in pairs, Gideon and Barak, Samson and Jephthah, and David and Samuel, in each case the second in history is the first in order of their listing. Those who "conquered kingdoms" would certainly include Gideon, conqueror of the Midianites (Judges 7), Barak over the Canaanites (Judges 4), Samson over the Philistines (Judges 14—16), Jephthah over the Ammonites (Judges 11), and David over the Philistines and other tribes (2 Samuel 5—21). Those leaders who administered righteously and justly received the blessings that God had promised.

Samson, David, and Daniel all "shut the mouths of lions" (Judges 14:5, 6; I Samuel 17:34, 35; Daniel 6:16-23). Of those who "quenched the fury of the flames," no example is more thrilling than the story of Daniel's friends, Shadrach, Meshach, and Abednego, who escaped the fire of Nebuchadnezzar's furnace (Daniel 3).

Those who "escaped the edge of the sword" would include, among others, David from Saul (1 Samuel 18:11; 19:10), Elijah from Jezebel (1 Kings 19:1-3), and Jeremiah from Jehoiakim (Jeremiah 36:19, 26). Those "whose weakness was turned to strength" are too numerous to mention. Those who "became powerful in battle" and "routed foreign armies" would refer to Joshua, the Judges, and David, and might possibly even apply to men of faith who lived in the intertestamental period of the Maccabees.

Certainly among the women who "received back their dead, raised to life again" would be the widow of Zarephath, whose son was restored by Elijah (1 Kings 17:17-24), and the Shunammite woman for whom Elisha performed the same miracle (2 Kings 4:17-37). An example in Jewish history of one who was "tortured" (put on a rack and beaten to death) was that of Eleazar, who lived at the time of Antiochus Epiphanes in the period of the Maccabees and was put to death in this manner because he would not deny his faith in God (2 Maccabees 6).

Joseph, Hanani, and Jeremiah could certainly be included among still others who suffered "jeers and floggings," and "were chained and put in prison." (See Genesis 39; 2 Chronicles 16:7-10; Jeremiah 37.)

The best example in the Old Testament of one who was "stoned" because of his faith was the righteous prophet Zechariah, who courageously delivered the word of the Lord to Joash, the idolatrous king of Judah (2 Chronicles 24:15-22). Jesus himself referred to this incident and to the stoning of prophets by the Jews (Matthew 23:35-37). Early in the history of the church, Stephen suffered the same fate at the hands of the enraged Jewish leaders to whom he preached and issued a call to repentance for their rejection and crucifixion of Christ (Acts 6:8—7:60).

There is a well-known Jewish tradition that Isaiah was "sawed in two" with a wooden saw during the reign of the wicked King Manasseh. Uriah, the prophet of Judah, was "put to death by the sword" by King Jehoiakim (Jeremiah 26:16-24), while the apostle James suffered martyrdom in the same manner at the hands of King Herod Agrippa I (Acts 12:1, 2).

Elijah and possibly Elisha would be among those who "went about in sheepskins and goatskins," were "destitute, persecuted, [and] mistreated," and who "wandered in deserts and mountains, and in caves and holes in the ground." (1 Kings 19:1-18; 2 Kings 1:7, 8). Their number would also include the prophets whom Obadiah hid from the judgment of Ahab and Jezebel (1 Kings 18:1-16), and the Maccabeans who fled during the persecution of Antiochus Epiphanes (2 Maccabees 5).

These great heroes of the past were contemptuously despised and rejected by a world that "was not worthy" of them. God, however, acknowledged and received them, for He "does not look at the things man looks at. Man looks at the outward appearance, but the Lord looks at the heart" (1 Samuel 16:7). They, like Paul, became "fools" (1 Corinthians 4:10) for the sake of their faith.

These witnesses of faith under the Old Covenant died without experiencing the ultimate promise of God, for its fulfillment awaited man's salvation through the death and resurrection of Jesus Christ. These men and women lived in a time in God's progressive program of revelation when it was more difficult to manifest and maintain faith in Him than it is for us today. It is to their credit that they looked forward in faith hundreds—even thousands—of years before He came. Moreover, since they placed their trust in God's promise of their future inheritance, they share even in our experiences under the New Covenant. Their role in God's eternal plan of redemption finds its completion in the glory and expansion of His kingdom. Their reward, though delayed, is not denied them.

Lessons From Chapter Eleven

Faith's Hall of Fame

There is a Baseball Hall of Fame in Cooperstown, New York. There is a Football Hall of Fame in Canton, Ohio. There is a Cowboy Hall of Fame in Oklahoma City. It is appropriate that there should also be Hall of Fame for Faith. We may picture this chapter as a gallery with portraits hung on the walls and short biographies beneath them. It is useful to look down the gallery and note the various kinds of people who lived triumphantly by faith. They are people of different eras. The list begins in Eden and ends with the king of Israel. The list includes men and women, commoners and kings, rich and poor, rural and urban, Jew and Gentile. The scenes are set in Eden, Chaldea, Canaan, and Egypt. The list includes a farmer, a carpenter, a shepherd, a prime minister, a general, a harlot, a judge, a prophet, and a king! They had almost nothing in common except faith; but that was the most important thing to have in common. Surely, it shows us that *we* can live by faith, whatever our nationality, geographic location, profession, or personal circumstances. If there were a modern day Hall of Fame for faith, would my picture be in it? Would yours?

Filing Under Chapter Eleven

There is a section of the business law of America that is commonly called "Chapter Eleven." The law provides for the business that needs to be reorganized. It provides protection from creditors until reorganization can be attained and the business become profitable once again. When a business applies for this reorganization process, it is said to be "filing under chapter eleven." All of us Christians are filing our lives under chapter eleven—Hebrews, chapter eleven. There is no other place to file our lives. There is no place to stand except on the promises and no way to live victoriously except to live by faith. Of course, living by faith involves an enormous reorganization of life. It is a reorganization of life that will make it vastly more profitable in an emotional and spiritual sense. It provides us protection from the debt of sin we've accumulated. Faith is filing under chapter eleven!

Faith and Sight

It has been said that only man comprehends what he cannot see and believes what he cannot comprehend. Much of what we comprehend we cannot see: atoms, germs, love, hate, loyalty, sacrifice. He who lives by sight lives very poorly indeed. Faith is learning to live by insight rather than by sight. Faith is not contrary to reason—it is beyond reason. We cannot always comprehend. Noah could not comprehend what the flood meant; nor Abel the eternal principles that underscored his sacrifice; nor Joseph his future greatness; nor Hagar her far-reaching influence. In fact, if we could comprehend all the sublime mysteries of life, we would not need faith. We could go by knowledge. But there is much that we cannot comprehend. We can only believe. We can believe intelligently, reasonably, thoughtfully; but we can only believe!

Faith and Fact

For centuries, the islands of New Zealand were unpopulated. No human being had ever set foot on them. Then the first settlers arrived, Polynesians from other Pacific islands. They sailed a thousand miles in outrigger canoes. They came with the purpose of settling there. How did they know there was land there? How did they know that they would not simply sail across empty seas till food and water ran out and they perished? They had known for generations that land was there because their voyagers had seen a long, white cloud on the distant horizon. They knew that when a cloud stayed in one place over a very long period of time there was land at that place. They called New Zealand the Land of the Long White Cloud.

Faith is like that. It is voyaging to an unseen land, journeying to an unknown future. But it is not mere guesswork, or chance, or superstition that is behind faith. There are facts behind faith, facts that suggest conclusions. Faith is not going against facts. Faith is not ignoring facts. Faith is taking facts and then going beyond them in the direction toward which they point!

Living by Faith

Everybody lives by faith in its ordinary and small sense. Whoever mails a letter lives by faith. Whoever gets on an airplane lives by faith. Whoever picks up a telephone lives by faith. Whoever plants a seed lives by faith. Since we *must* live by faith if we live at all, how is it we cannot translate that into spiritual things? How is it that we cannot see that the larger things of life must be dealt with just as we deal with the little things of life? No one can make you feel inferior because you live by faith. So does he. Everyone does. There is no other way to live!

CHAPTER TWELVE

Added Warnings to Faithfulness

Hebrews 12:1-29

The Christian Race (12:1-3)

After enumerating the examples of Old Covenant saints who maintained confidence in God in spite of persecution and affliction, the author of Hebrews again admonished his readers to persevere in the conflict of their faith. He used the image of the athletic arena as he called on them to run their course with patience.

The "cloud of witnesses" looking down on their spiritual race was composed of the roll call of the faithful mentioned in the previous chapter. It is interesting to think how their number has increased since this Scripture was written. The author may have been trying to point out that the concerned observation of these faithful witnesses of the past was a natural outgrowth of their preparatory part in God's eternal program of revelation. They were anxiously watching as they saw the results of their faith demonstrated in the life and labors of the church. Unlike "popcorn" spectators at an entertainment event, these observers had a genuine stake in the faithfulness of the Hebrew Christians, as well as later generations of believers.

His purpose in mentioning the "cloud of witnesses," on the other hand, may simply have been to encourage his readers by the example of those who had gone before them. The fact that the word used for "witness" in Hebrews 12:1 is the same word from which the English *martyr* is derived might add strength to this conclusion.

Perhaps both of the foregoing ideas are implied in the context of this Scripture. A Christian should be encouraged by looking to the victorious examples of the witnesses from the past, and by realizing that these witnesses are looking to him to fulfill the promised redemption of God for which they, under the Old Covenant, had prepared.

The garb of participation in the Christian race must be free of excess weight. The spiritual runner is to disregard any hindrance, care, possession, and side interest that would impede him in his course. Above all, Christians must guard against sin, which clings and ensnares and will inevitably cause them to stumble in their running if it is not removed. There is honest disagreement between students of this book over whether the writer was referring to sin in general or to a specific besetting sin that individual Christians may experience. The original language of the Greek would tend to support the former explanation.

Another key to victory for the Christian runner is to fix his eyes on Jesus, the trailblazer of our faith as well as its completer and chief encouragement. In one sense, all faith in God has had its beginning in, and has been directed toward, Jesus Christ, who existed prior to all history. From the very beginning, faith has been the only means by which man has been acceptably related to God, and that faith has been ultimately directed toward God's promise in Christ. (See Genesis 3:15; 1 Corinthians 10:4; Hebrews 7:15; 11:26.)

In the life, death, and resurrection of Christ, faith found its most complete expression and realization. He has, indeed, run the perfect race before us. He was, even above all the saints mentioned and alluded to in Hebrews 11, the great exemplar of faith. Ignoring the disgrace and suffering of the cross, and looking to the true and ultimate reward of faith, Jesus maintained absolute trust in God and patiently endured crucifixion. His faith was wondrously vindicated in His glorious exaltation "at the right hand of the throne of God." (See Hebrews 2:9-18; 5:6-9; 8:1; and 10:12.) Likewise, Christ will perfect the faith of His followers who place their confidence in Him. He is the beginning and end of their faith. The readers of the epistle are admonished to consider their experience in the light of His example and be encouraged by His victory. He will surely complete any good works begun in the lives of His children. How can one who looks to Jesus be weary and disheartened?

God's Discipline of His Sons (12:4-13)

In verse 4, the author called attention to the fact that, in all their sufferings, his readers had not faced death in resistance of sin, as did Christ and many of the children of God. He reminds the Hebrew Christians of the words of Proverbs 3:11, 12, that one is not to regard lightly, or despair at, the discipline of God. A lack of discipline by a father is taken as a lack of love. Every father who loves his son corrects and punishes him when it is necessary.

To receive and accept correction and reproof is to assume the role of a true son. To be denied or to reject control and chastisement is to play the part of an illegitimate child and be refused the privileges of a son. To escape discipline, then, is no mark of favor.

If we reverence our earthly fathers, how much more respect and subordination should we have for the control of our Heavenly Father, who is the Creator of imperishable life? Their discipline of "a little while," until we reach adulthood, is limited to their own judgment, which is subject to error. God's perfect and divine discipline is always for our eternal good and spiritual welfare that we might share in His holiness.

It is the nature of any chastisement that it seems painful and bitter when it is experienced. Divine correction, however, always produces the fruit of righteousness and peace in those who accept it and are spiritually responsive to it. A sign of immaturity in a believer is his inability or unwillingness to see beyond a chastisement to the good that will result from it. The difference between a sinner and a Christian is not what happens to them, but their reactions and attitudes toward it when it comes. A child of God interprets adversity in an entirely different light from that of an unbeliever. Realizing this eternal truth, we can understand and heed the words of Paul, James, Peter, and others who have told us to rejoice even in our sufferings (Colossians 1:23, 24; James 1:2-4; I Peter 1:6-9; 4:12-16).

The writer wanted his readers to understand that chastisement was a necessary part of the believer's spiritual education and that their adversities could bring beneficial results. He exhorted them to "strengthen [their] feeble arms and weak knees" and "make level paths for [their] feet." (Similar images are used in Isaiah 35:3 and Proverbs 4:26.) Their own spiritual welfare and especially that of some of their palsied and fainthearted members who were in danger of going astray depended on it. A lame Christian will falter in a church that staggers in its faith, but he will experience spiritual healing in a body of believers who are moving in a straightforward course. Weaker brethren always need the help of the more robust Christians.

Spiritual Responsibility in the Church (12:14-17)

In order for the church to move forward in the manner suggested, the members were admonished to exhibit a spirit of peace and harmony toward each other and outsiders. In addition, their lives were to be characterized by consecration and devotion. Such sanctification opens the eyes so that one can see God; without it, no one will behold Him. (See Matthew 5:8, 9; Romans 12:1, 2.)

In pursuing a course of peace and purity, the Hebrew Christians were further exhorted to give diligent heed to their number so that none of them would fall back. Possibly some were in danger of losing their devotion, having their spiritual vision blurred, and falling from the grace of God. It was the responsibility of the church to help prevent that from happening.

If the church lacked tranquillity and holiness, and failed to exercise careful scrutiny over its members, there could arise among them individuals who would cause difficulty and bring destruction. Even one such corrupt and sinful person could defile the body of Christ like a poisonous weed that spreads its poison to the environment around it and endangers the whole garden. The reference to sexual immorality is probably a literal reference, but may also imply spiritual adultery, such as idolatry or apostasy. (See Judges 2:17.) Faith and life, doctrine and morals, are directly related. No one walks close to God and close to the world at the same time. When consecration recedes, moral decay sets in.

Surely one of the most damnable sins among the people of God is that of profanity. This evil is by no means limited to taking God's name in vain or using foul language. It is a matter of treating any spiritual thing as if it were common or ordinary. Esau is mentioned as the cardinal example from the Old Testament of a profane person. For a mere mess of pottage, he sold his birthright as the firstborn of his father's house. This birthright carried with it the main inheritance, the headship of the family, and the preservation of the family name. In its worst sense, his action represented lack of faith in God's promise to Abraham and his heirs. To assuage his temporary hunger, Esau sold his permanent blessing. To satisfy an immediate physical desire, he bargained his future God-given inheritance. The tears of remorse that came later could not recover than which he had forfeited so lightly and irresponsibly for the moment. (See Genesis 25:29-34; 27:1-40).

Profanity represents a tragic loss of spiritual values. It is the lowering of the Heavenly to the mundane. Every child of God should shun it like the plague. Profanity can be considered no less than spiritual suicide. It represents a lack of faith in God and ultimately manifests itself in apostasy.

The Mountains of the Two Covenants (12:18-24)

The writer of Hebrews continued his exhortation to perseverance on the part of his readers by drawing an imaginative and stirring contrast between the Old and New Covenant orders. These are represented in the earthly Mount Sinai and the Heavenly Mount Zion respectively. The inauguration of the Old Covenant on Sinai was marked by marvelous physical manifestations of God's power. The mountain was wonderfully clothed with fire, blackness, and tempest. To touch it, or even approach it, was fatal. At the sound of the trumpet and the voice of God, the people were so terrified that they fell back and pleaded for Moses to intercede so that God would not speak to them personally. Their fear had been magnified all the more by God's instructions that an animal that contacted the mountain was not to be touched, but was to be stoned or "shot with arrows" from a safe distance. Even Moses became afraid and shook. (See Exodus 19:10-19; 20:18-21; Deuteronomy 4:11, 12, 36; Acts 7:32.)

All of these miraculous sights and sounds that were associated with the giving of the Old Testament law and that played such an important role in the history and background of the Jewish faith and heritage were observable by the five senses. To the Hebrews writer, any tendency to glorify these or similar extraordinary physical displays, with a desire to return to what they represented or that with which they were associated, was simply a mark of spiritual immaturity. The mature Christian desires to perceive in the realm of the Spirit without depending on the crutch of outward physical manifestations to bolster his faith. This great lesson is one that the church in every age seems to have difficulty learning and applying. Ours is no exception.

The mount to which the author said his readers under the New Covenant had come was not a place that could be seen and touched physically and that overwhelmed the five senses. It was Mount Zion (the hill on which the temple and Jerusalem were built, Psalm 78:68-72; Isaiah 40:9), a shadow of the Heavenly city. (See Revelation 14:1). He was, of course, not implying that they had already entered Heaven, that "new Jerusalem" that John saw (Revelation 21:2). Rather, he was reaffirming one of the great themes of Hebrews: through the eyes of faith, we can enter the presence of God through Jesus Christ. Although the full joys of habitation in the Heavenly city must await the life to come, the believer is spiritually already a citizen of that great community. As such, he bears kinship to the hosts of angels who reside there.

Some students of Hebrews believe that the "joyful assembly" refers not to the "angels" of verse 22, but to the "church" of verse 23. This assembly and "the church of the firstborn, whose names are written in heaven," they say refer to those under the Old Covenant who lived and died in faith. Others, however, suggest that the "spirits of righteous men made perfect" are the saints of the past. They consider the "church of the firstborn" to be the community of all living believers. There are many references in the New Testament to Christians being enrolled in God's book of life (Philippians 4:3; Revelation 21:27).

In that Heavenly city to which we come by faith is "God, the judge of all." (See 4:13; 10:30, 31, 36, and 37 for other references in the letter to the judgment of God.) Also present, as the readers were reminded many times in this great book, is Jesus, the mediator of the New Covenant, and His blood, which accomplishes what even righteous Abel's could not. While the latter's blood could only cry out for vengeance (Genesis 4:10), the sacrifice of Christ brings complete forgiveness of sin.

The Voice of God (12:25-29)

Repeating an admonition similar to those that he gave in 2:1-3 and 10:28, 29, the Hebrews writer warned his Christian readers not to refuse to heed God's voice. Their Jewish ancestors had been guilty of this during the wilderness experiences under Moses and, indeed, throughout all their history. If the judgment of God was firm against those who rejected His revelation at Sinai, how much more certain and fearful will it be against those who forsake the word given from the Heavenly Mount Zion!

Quoting Haggai 2:6, he contrasted the temporary nature of the Old Covenant order, symbolized by the shaking of the earthly mount, with the New Covenant kingdom, which will remain firm even in the day of God's promised final shaking of both heaven and earth. In that day, the visible, shadowy, impermanent world will be removed, but the eternal, spiritual kingdom of the Heavenly city will remain forever.

With the realization that they were blessed to be a part of God's everlasting kingdom, which will stand firm when all of the kingdoms of this world have passed away, the Hebrew Christians were admonished to serve Him gratefully in reverence and awe. It is a high privilege to be numbered among God's people, a privilege that demands that we "be grateful." It is not a privilege to be taken lightly or for granted. Our God is merciful, gracious, and kind, but He is also "a consuming fire" (Deuteronomy 4:24) in His judgment against those who reject His Word and refuse His warnings.

Lessons From Chapter Twelve

All for Jesus

Who has not been inspired by the familiar hymn, "All for Jesus"?

> All for Jesus! All for Jesus!
> All my being's ransomed powers.
> All my thoughts and words and doings,
> All my days and all my hours.

Hebrews, chapter 12, has a similar theme. For Jesus, we lift up our all: our hands, our eyes, and our feet.

Lift Up Your Feet (v. 1)

There are three bits of advice in Hebrews 12:1 about lifting up our feet. We are to lay aside the weights; we are to run with perseverance; and we are to run on the proper path.

The first is illustrated in an event reported two or three years ago in the St. *Petersburg (Florida) Times.* A young man was driving his 1971 Porsche to work when the car caught fire. He watched it burn to a cinder. He said of that car, "It meant everything to me." Even if we make some allowance for the inexact use of language of youth, the statement is startling. If your car means *everything* to you, you're a pagan. If your career means *everything* to you, you're a pagan. If your family means *everything* to you, you've forgotten something. If health means *everything* to you, you've forgotten something. If life itself means *everything* to you, you've forgotten something. *Christ* must mean everything to us! He is quite content for all of the above to mean *something* to us, but not *everything.*

The second way to lift up our feet is with patience or perseverance. A French proverb says, "Laziness is often mistaken for patience." We are not running a fifty-yard dash. We are in an endurance race.

The third important advice from this chapter is we are to be running in the right direction. What could be plainer than this: "Let us run… the race marked out for us"? If you get on the wrong track, you'll never finish the race!

Lift Up Your Eyes (v. 2)

We are to lift up our eyes that we may see Jesus. There is an old story that goes something like this. A man once found a five-dollar bill. After that, he always looked down when he walked. Over the course of the years, he found twelve hair pins, five paper clips, a ball point pen, one nickel, four pennies, and a very large assortment of gum wrappers. But during those years, he never saw a flower, a tree, or the smile of a passing stranger! If we just look down at our problems, we will never succeed. We will be like the centipede. He was doing fine until someone asked him which of his one hundred legs came after which. He'd never thought of that before. The more he thought about it, the more he couldn't remember, and he found he couldn't walk at all! Lift up your eyes from the problems at your feet! Look up to Jesus.

According to verse three, looking unto Jesus will keep us from being faint in our minds. The original recipients of this letter were apt to experience persecution. It would be easy for such suffering Christians to conclude that they had been forsaken by God. Looking to Jesus would remind them that suffering is not an indication of abandonment, but a characteristic of Sonship. If God's only begotten Son suffered, are we, his later sons, to be exempt from it? When you suffer, never suppose that it means God doesn't like you. See it as the hallmark of sonship.

Lift Up Your Hands (v. 12)

Often, when we are tempted to give up, we say, "I throw up my hands," which means, "I surrender." The gesture that accompanies "throwing up our hands" is usually just the opposite. Our hands drop down at our sides in utter futility and failure. Christ wants to encourage us. He says to us, as He said to His disciples long ago, "Be of good cheer. I have overcome the world."

The great hero of the book of Acts is not Paul. It is Barnabas. Paul had gone home to Tarsus discouraged and defeated. We assume that the brilliant preacher was simply making tents again.

But Barnabas saw at Antioch an opportunity for Paul. He went to Tarsus and brought Paul to Antioch. Paul worked there effectively for a whole year, and from Antioch went out on the first of the great missionary journeys. But none of that would have happened without Barnabas. Is it any wonder the Bible calls him "Son of Encouragement"? We might have called him "Mr. Encourager"!

We are to lift up our hands and to lift up the hands of others as well. There is every reason to be encouraged about Christianity. We must lift up the hands that hang down. Someone has said that faith is not trying to believe something in spite of the evidence. It is daring to do something in spite of the consequences!

CHAPTER THIRTEEN

Faith at Work

Hebrews 13:1-25

Brotherly Love and Purity of Life (13:1-6)

The author of Hebrews completed his marvelous and irrefutable argument for the superiority of the New Covenant over the Old, and of the eternal reality of the unseen world over the unreal and transitory nature of the physical world in the first twelve chapters. The final chapter was designed to conclude this wonderful letter with an exhortation to his readers to fulfill certain obligations that needed special attention in their situation. In the previous chapter, he issued a call for harmony and purity among them. Here, he spelled out in greater detail the life and conduct that he had in mind.

Although the fellowship of these believers was already characterized by brotherly love (6:10; 10:33, 34), it was a virtue that needed encouragement so that it might not weaken and grow cold. The admonition for them to "continue" in it was a reminder of the new commandment that Christ had given His followers, that they love one another as He loved had them (John 13:34; 15:12). John reiterated that idea forcefully in his first epistle (1 John 2:7-11; 3:14-16; 4:7-11, 20, 21), and Paul warmly commended the Thessalonians for practicing it so wonderfully in their fellowship (1 Thessalonians 4:9, 10). Certainly the church of Jesus Christ, above all others, needs to know and appreciate the words of Psalm 133:1: "How good and pleasant it is when brothers live together in unity!"

Such love regards hospitality to Christian strangers, perhaps those fleeing persecution or merely traveling, as a blessed privilege as well as a sacred responsibility. Abraham and Lot, thinking that they were merely entertaining visiting men of God, had unknowingly hosted angels from Heaven (Genesis 18:1-21; 19:1-22). Whether or not we can expect such experiences as these, anyone who practices genuine hospitality will soon realize that the blessings he receives from such contacts are far greater than those he bestows.

Their brotherly love was also to find expression in compassion and care for those who had endured imprisonment and adversity. Echoing Paul's words to the Corinthians, that all other members were to suffer with any part of the body that suffered (1 Corinthians 12:26), this admonition speaks of an intense vicarious suffering, almost as if the sympathizer had experienced the same grief himself. Of course, the words of this text need to be read against the background that in those days prisoners received little beyond what friends brought them. Be that as it may, the principle is universally true that in the church there is little room for passive pity, only for strong involvement in the painful experiences of a brother.

The writer also gave attention to the moral conduct of the church members. In a world in which family life was little esteemed, sexual promiscuity and adultery were rampant, and prostitution was part of ceremonial practice in certain religions, these Christians were admonished to honor marriage and refrain from fornication and adultery. Marriage is ordained of God, and its purity must be maintained. Those who violate it and engage in sexual sinning will not escape the judgment of God. (See 1 Corinthians 6:9, 10; Galatians 5:19-21.)

The thought and life of the Christian is also to be free of greed. Jesus taught that one cannot serve God and money (Matthew 6:24), and Paul affirmed that "the love of money is a root of all kinds of evil" (1 Timothy 6:10; see also 1 Timothy 3:3). We are to be satisfied with what we have, trusting in God's promise to provide for us and protect us no matter what life may offer or what men might try to do to us (Psalm 118:6). Like Paul, we must learn "to be content whatever the circumstances." The secret lies in having the confidence that we "can do everything through him who gives [us] strength" (Philippians 4:11-13), and in realizing the fact that "if God is for us, who can be against us?" (Romans 8:31).

Leaders to Follow and Sacrifices to Offer (13:7-17)

In pursuing godly lives, the Hebrew Christians had the worthy example of those leaders (perhaps apostles, elders, teachers, and deacons) who brought God's Word to them and exemplified it in their faith and manner of life. Some of them may have been included in those to whom reference was made in Hebrews 2:1-4. Virtuous as was the behavior of these honored men of the past, though, persecution and heresy had since come. The circumstances surrounding the readers were changing.

In all of the changing conditions of life, however, there is One who remains eternally the same: Jesus Christ. He never changes. The church does not depend on its past leaders for its continuity. Even the strength of their example lies in their faith in the unchanging Christ. The message concerning Him to which they committed themselves remains constant. He makes available to all of His children, in every age, the same strength, courage, and direction. Our faith is grounded in the eternity of our Lord and the unchangeableness of His being. He is, indeed, "the same yesterday and today and forever."

Since Christ is eternally the same, one who trusts in Him will not be swept about by strange teachings concerning nonessentials. Our strength lies in the grace of God (2 Corinthians 12:9), not in the opinions of men concerning what meats should or should not be eaten. Those who have been obsessed with opinionated views about food have profited little from it and have often introduced division and false doctrine into the body of Christ. (See Romans 14; 1 Corinthians 8; 10:18-33; Colossians 2:16.)

Over against the question of eating certain foods that in themselves have no part in essential doctrine, the author of this letter referred to the Christian altar, that is, the sacrifice of Christ, which is the antitype of the sacrificial atonement bull and goat. Even the priests who served in the tabernacle could not eat of those animal sacrifices, for they were burned completely outside the camp of Israel (Leviticus 16:27). The believer, however, can by faith feed spiritually on Jesus Christ, the ultimate sacrifice to which all of the atonement offerings pointed. In fact, the spiritual nourishment that comes through Him is all that really counts for eternity. Although this text may not refer directly to the Lord's Supper, an indirect application to it most certainly can be made. (See also John 6:26-58.) The Christian thus has a sin offering of which those who still belong to the Old Covenant cannot partake. They who persist in observing its sacrificial regulations deny the all-sufficient sacrifice of Christ and deprive themselves of the spiritual nourishment that is found in Him.

Fulfilling the prophetic typology of the atonement sacrifices and possibly also the sin offering of the red heifer for purification (Numbers 19:1-10), even to the place outside the camp where they were burned, Jesus Christ was crucified beyond the gate of Jerusalem for the forgiveness of our sins and the cleansing of our consciences. (See Hebrews 10.) Hebrews 13:13, along with John 19:17, 20, 41, is used by many students of the New Testament to support their contention that Gordon's Calvary, located about 250 yards northeast of the Damascus Gate and clearly beyond the walls of Jerusalem as they existed in the time of Christ, was the site of the crucifixion.

The crucifixion of Jesus outside Jerusalem marvelously symbolized His rejection by the Jewish community and their separation of themselves from His sacrifice and the new order that centered in Him. It also pointed out the inescapable truth that any Jew who wanted to receive the offering of Christ had to come outside the pales of the Jewish system and leave its sacrificial regulations behind. The New Covenant relationship is not merely a piece of new cloth on an old garment or new wine in old wineskins (Matthew 9:16,

17). It is a new order entirely, and for one to be a part of it, he had to leave the old order as a necessary and binding way of life. (For a more detailed study of this truth, see Acts 15:1-31 and Galatians 1—6.)

Accordingly, the readers of this letter were admonished to follow "him outside the camp," sharing with Him the abuse and shame of the cross. (See Deuteronomy 21:22, 23; Galatians 3:13; and 1 Corinthians 1:18-25.) Leaving the earthly Jerusalem, that is, the fleshly religion it represented, they were to fix their eyes on the Heavenly Jerusalem, the "city with foundations," yet to come. The same could be said to anyone who is inclined to hold back from complete surrender to the cross of Christ because of earthly relationships, institutional attachments, social life, family relationships, personal friendships, and so forth. He calls us to "know Christ, and the power of his resurrection and the fellowship of sharing in his sufferings, becoming like him in his death" (Philippians 3:10).

Since Jesus has paid the supreme and perfect sacrifice of His blood outside the camp for our sins, the only sacrifices with which we please God are those of praise and thanksgiving to Him and the benevolent sharing of our goods and possessions with others. (See Micah 6:8; Matthew 22:37-39; Romans 12:1; Galatians 6:10; and James 1:27.) The keynotes of our sacrifice to God are gratitude, reverence, and awe (Hebrews 12:28).

These Hebrew Christians already had been urged to remember the worthy example of their past leaders. They were further admonished to obey and submit themselves to their present elders, realizing that they bore a sacred responsibility to God for the care of the souls in the church entrusted to them. With proper respect, they could joyfully fulfill this responsibility. Rejection and resentment of their discipline, however, would bring grief to them as leaders and disadvantage to the whole church.

Final Exhortations and Blessings (13:18-25)

The closing words of this epistle contain an earnest request by the author for intercessory prayer on his behalf. This was based on the clear conscience of his honest life, and/or possibly the sincerity and truth of this letter, and his strong desire to revisit them soon. Apparently, he had been associated with them before and had possibly exercised a position of leadership among them. He gave no clear indication of what was preventing his speedy return to them.

There follows a benedictory intercession for them, addressed to "the God of peace" to equip them to do His will as they worked to please Him. The sacrifice of God's Son had removed the ultimate barrier to peace, sin. Only by faith in Him can one experience the confidence and assurance of salvation that brings eternal peace. (See John 14:27; 16:33; Romans 5:1; 8:6; Galatians 5:22; Ephesians 2:14-17.)

This context contains the only reference in the epistle to the resurrection of our Lord. The major emphasis throughout the book has been the cross and the exaltation of Christ in relation to His high priestly ministry. Here the author significantly noted that by raising Jesus, the "great Shepherd of the sheep," from the dead, God marvelously demonstrated His acceptance of the sacri-rice of Christ and His blood by which the new and everlasting covenant was confirmed and on which it is based. We have here also the only reference in the letter to Christ as a shepherd. (See Isaiah 63:11 and John 10:11-18.)

The Hebrew Christians were asked to receive the the letter and read it carefully and patiently, for the author considered it to be a short treatment of a very important and profound subject. (See Hebrews 5:11; 9:5.) He also informed them that when he came, he hoped to see them in company with Timothy, who had been recently released from prison and was, in all probability, the frequent companion of Paul.

The greeting that the writer asked his readers to convey to their rulers and to "all God's people" would suggest that the recipients of the letter were probably a part of a larger community of Christians. Perhaps they were a single group within a city of believers, and the leaders (or some of them) were possibly over the larger body and not numbered among them. (See the number of separate groups of believers in Rome that Paul greeted in Romans 16:3-15.) The salutation sent from the "those of Italy" could refer to people residing in Italy or to Italian Christians living abroad who wished to send a message to their friends at home. It is conceivable that the author may refer to Italians living away from home who were greeting fellow exiles residing elsewhere. No clear conclusion can be drawn from this greeting concerning the place from which the letter was written or the people to whom it was addressed.

Although the final benediction is shorter than most of those in Paul's writings (Titus 3:15 excepted), it is one frequently used in the New Testament. What better way could the writer of Hebrews have closed his splendid treatise than with the simple blessing, "Grace be with you all"?

Lessons From Chapter Thirteen

Love Is a Many Splendored Thing

That is the title of a once-popular song. Some think it should be changed to "Love Is a Many Splintered Thing." Maybe that's because they got stuck by some of the splinters! Maybe it's because our love gets splintered off in several directions. There are, after all, many claims on our affection. We sometimes feel we are crippled because so many different Greek words are all translated "love" in English. On the other hand, it does serve to illustrate that the claims for our heart are many. In this text, there are four forces that make a claim upon our affection. Some are mutually beneficial, and some are mutually destructive. You need to know something about each one.

Your Fellow Man Makes a Claim on Your Affection

'In the state of Oklahoma, the highways carry a sign: "Drive Friendly." We ought to put a sign like that along the highways of life: "Live Friendly." Someone once said, "It's nice to be important, but it's more important to be nice."

Brotherly love always makes us think of Philadelphia, Pennsylvania, the City of Brotherly Love. And that is the very word that is found in the Greek version of Hebrews 12:1: "Philadelphia." There is not only a Philadelphia in Pennsylvania; there is also a Philadelphia in the Bible. It is one of the cities to which the seven letters in the Book of Revelation were sent. It got its name from Attalus II, whose loyalty to his brother Eumanes II made him famous. He had the opportunity to unseat his brother and take his power. He lived in an age when such things were commonly done. But Attalus remained firmly loyal and devoted to his brother and a town in Turkey was named for his brotherly love.

Your Mate Makes a Claim for Your Affection

What's new about that? Nothing. What's significant about it is that it is an exclusive claim on your affections. At least it makes an exclusive claim on a certain kind of affection! You can still have brotherly love, regardless of the gender of the person! But marital love is exclusive. A young engaged couple were buying wedding rings. He tried his on. "It's too tight," he said. "It will cut off the circulation." She replied, "It'll cut off the circulation no matter how big it is!" Truly, marriage must cut off one's circulation!

Verse four has two sides, like a coin. Not everybody sees both sides. The ugliness of sexual sins should never make us think that sex is ugly. The loveliness of sex in marriage should never make us think that sin is lovely! Sometimes it seems that those who speak the loudest against sex outside of marriage are really against sex altogether. To them God says, "Marriage is honorable in all, and the bed undefiled" (Hebrews 13:4, KJV). You can't get much plainer than that! On the other hand, there are those who recognize that sex is one of the good things God created but do not recognize that God limited it to marriage. They think that since sex is a good thing, it cannot be bad. To them, God says that He will certainly judge (punish) those who commit such sins. You can't get much plainer than that! If there is any confusion on these matters, it is not because God doesn't speak plainly and unequivocally!

Money Makes a Claim for Your Affection

Covetousness is the Biblical word for the love of money. When John D. Rockefeller was the richest man in the world, someone asked him how much money was enough. He replied, "Just a little bit more." The love of money is the most subtle sin in the world: easy to do, hard to recognize, hard to resist.

Why does it come up here in this chapter, seemingly out of place? Because it is destructive of the two earlier loves. If you don't think money is destructive of love for your fellowman, go into business with a friend. Or lend money to a friend. The friendship between Jesus and Judas was neither the first nor the last to be ruined by money. Someone has said, "If you really want to find out how much your children love each other, die without a will!" Everybody knows an example of a family that has been broken into pieces because of money. It is likely that the first quarrel you ever had with a tiny playmate was over a possession. Think about the last quarrel you had. It was probably over a possession!

Money is destructive of that other love already discussed, marital love. Sometimes it is the presence of money and sometimes it is the absence of money. Recently, a millionaire auto dealer in Tampa, Florida, was shot to death by his wife. She shot him in the back six times "in self-defense." When they arrested her, she said, "It's all because of the money. I wish there had never been any money at all!"

Joe Louis said, "I don't like money, actually. It just quiets my nerves!"

Many have found money to be exactly the opposite. How sad is the definition of love inherent in this little commercial jingle used by a bank in Washington, D.C.

> Who's gonna love you when you're old and gray.
> Put a little love away.
>
> Everybody needs a penny for a rainy day.
> Put a little love away.

The Master Makes a Claim for Your Affection

He is our helper (v. 6). He is faithful and never changes (v. 8). He suffered for us (v. 12). He deserves our affection (v. 13). He deserves our praise (v. 15). He deserves our sacrificial offerings (v. 16). He deserves our obedience (v. 17).

Your response to the Master will affect your response to all those other claims upon your love. It will sanctify your friendship and make your love of fellowman something to be cherished, never something to be exploited. It will sanctify your marriage so that every part is holy. A marriage is never a two-person parternship. It is a three-person partnership. That's why Ecclesiastes 4:12 cal}s the marriage bond a "cord of *three* strands." It is not a cord of two strands. God is the third strand in the tie, the third person in the partnership.

Your response to the Master's claim for your love will determine whether you can resist the call of money upon your love. Long ago, Jesus said, "You cannot serve both God and Money" (Matthew 6:24). Money and the Master have been rivals for your affection since the first coin was minted.

The sun is 865,000 miles across; but the smallest coin can block out the sun if you hold it close enough to your eye! Our Great God can be blocked from view by a very small amount of money! If you honor the Master's claim for your affection, He will enrich your love for fellow man and family; and He will save you from the love of money! This statement from C.S. Lewis comes to mind:

> To love at all is to be vulnerable. Love anything, and your heart will certainly be wrung and possibly broken. If you want to make sure of keeping it intact, you must give your heart to no one, not even to an animal. Wrap it carefully round with hobbies and little luxuries; avoid all entanglements; lock it up safe in the casket or coffin of your selfishness. But in that casket—safe, dark, motionless, air-less—it will change. It will not be broken; it will become unbreakable, impenetrable, irredeemable... The only place outside Heaven where you can be perfectly safe from all the dangers ... of love is Hell.[2]

---

[2] C.S. Lewis, *The Four Loves* (New York: Harcourt, Brace & World, Inc., [Harcourt Brace Jovanovich, Inc.] © 1960 by Helen Joy Lewis), p. 169.

ABOUT THE AUTHOR

David L. Eubanks, Ph.D., has been the president of Johnson Bible College since 1969. Before taking that position he was a professor at the college for over ten years. Among the classes he taught was a semester course on Hebrews. He has traveled extensively, visiting churches and missionaries, preaching and teaching throughout the United States and in nineteen foreign countries. He has also authored numerous religious articles and devotional materials.

Robert C. Shannon was minister of First Christian Church, Largo, Florida, for eighteen years. For eight years he served as a missionary behind the Iron Curtain. He also was a Professor of Preaching at Atlanta Christian College for a number of years. He has authored or co-authored twelve books and lectured at twenty-six colleges and seminaries.

Printed in the United States
24391LVS00006B/261

9 781414 041100